# PREFACES TO HISTORY

# PREFACES TO
# HISTORY

## BRUCE CATTON

1970

DOUBLEDAY & COMPANY, INC., GARDEN CITY, NEW YORK

Grateful acknowledgment is made to the following for their copyrighted material:

AMERICAN HERITAGE PUBLISHING CO., INC.

For the following articles and reviews which appeared in *American Heritage* magazine: "For an Emotional Understanding," June 1956; "Morning Star," February 1958; "Aristotle and Pandora," August 1959; "Setting the Pattern," June 1961; "The Men Who Made Canoes," February 1965; "The Swordbearers," April 1965; "The Dreadful Noise," April 1967; "Jeff Davis: The Man Behind the Image," June 1967; "A World of Wonder," April 1959; "The Great American Game," April 1959. All by Bruce Catton.

NELSON DOUBLEDAY, INC.

For the Introduction by Bruce Catton to a special edition of *John Brown's Body*, by Stephen Vincent Benét. Copyright © 1969 by Nelson Doubleday, Inc.

HARCOURT, BRACE & WORLD, INC.

For "A New Appraisal," by Bruce Catton. Copyright © 1958 by Harcourt, Brace & World, Inc. Reprinted from *Sherman, Fighting Prophet*, by Lloyd Lewis.

HOUGHTON MIFFLIN COMPANY

For the Introduction by Bruce Catton to *The Battle of Gettysburg*, by Frank A. Haskell.

INDIANA UNIVERSITY PRESS

For Foreword by Bruce Catton to *Prince Napoleon in America, 1861*, by Camille Ferri Pisani.

ILLINOIS STATE HISTORICAL LIBRARY

For article, "The End of the Centennial," by Bruce Catton, which appears in *A Portion of That Field* (University of Illinois Press, 1967).

MICHIGAN HISTORICAL COMMISSION

For "Our American Heritage," *Michigan History, XLVII* (December, 1964, pp. 369–372). Written by Bruce Catton.

NORTHWESTERN UNIVERSITY PRESS

For "The Generalship of Ulysses S. Grant," by Bruce Catton, in *Grant, Lee, Lincoln and the Radicals*, edited by Grady McWhiney.

THE SATURDAY EVENING POST COMPANY

For "The Real Michigan," by Bruce Catton. Reprinted with the permission of *Holiday*, © 1957 by The Curtis Publishing Company.

# CONTENTS

## CONTENTS

# PREFACES TO HISTORY

# Preface to *The Army of the Potomac* Trilogy*

## 1962

The books which make up this trilogy began, very simply, as an attempt to understand the men who fought in the Army of the Potomac. As a small boy I had known a number of these men in their old age; they were grave, dignified, and thoughtful, with long white beards and a general air of being pillars of the community. They lived in rural Michigan in the pre-automobile age, and for the most part they had never been fifty miles away from the farm or the dusty village streets; yet once, ages ago, they had been everywhere and had seen everything, and nothing that happened to them thereafter meant anything much. All that was real had taken place when they were young; everything after that had simply been a process of waiting for death, which did not frighten them much—they had seen it inflicted in the worst possible way on boys who had not bargained for it, and they had enough of the old-fashioned religion to believe without any question that when they passed over they would simply be rejoining men and ways of living which they had known long ago.

This was too much for an adolescent to understand. Per-

* *Mr. Lincoln's Army, Glory Road, A Stillness at Appomattox,* by Bruce Catton, Doubleday & Company, Inc., 1962

haps it is too much for anybody to understand, in a skeptical
age. But there it was: these old gentlemen, drowsing out
the greater part of their lives in the backwoods, had once
been lifted beyond themselves by an experience which perhaps was all the more significant because it was imperfectly
understood. They gave a tone and a color to the lives of
the people who knew them, and they put a special meaning
on such a word as "patriotism"; it was not something you
talked about very much, just a living force that you instinc-
tively responded to. I can remember one old man who had
lost his left arm in the Wilderness, and he used to go about
town in the summer peddling cherries and blackberries
in a bucket—there was just enough of his left forearm so
that he could hook it over the bail of the bucket and carry
it conveniently—and it never once entered my childish
head to feel sorry for him because he had been a cripple
for half a century. On the contrary, I thought he was rather
lucky. He carried with him forever the visible sign that he
had fought for his country and had been wounded in its
service. Probably only a very backward boy could have
thought anything of the kind.

Still, that was what it was like. A generation grew up
in the shadow of a war which, because of its distance,
somehow had lost all resemblance to everyday reality. To
a generation which knew the war only by hearsay, it seemed
that these aged veterans had been privileged to know the
greatest experience a man could have. We saw the Civil
War, in other words, through the distorting haze of endless
Decoration Day reminiscences; to us it was a romantic business because all we ever got a look at was the legend built
up through fifty years of peace.

We do learn as we grow older, and eventually I realized
that this picture was somewhat out of focus. War, obviously,
is the least romantic of all of man's activities, and it contains
elements which the veterans do not describe to children.
This aged berry-peddler, for instance, who lost his arm in

the Wilderness: he had never told me about the wounded men who were burned to death in the forest fire which swept that infernal stretch of woodland while the battle was going on; nor had any of his comrades who survived that fight and went on through the whole campaign to the last days at Petersburg ever mentioned the lives that were wasted by official blunders, the dirt and the war-weariness and the soul-numbing disillusionment that came when it seemed that what they were doing was going for nothing. There was a deacon in the church, who used to remind us proudly that he had served in the 2nd Ohio Cavalry. Not until years later did I learn that this regiment had gone with Sheridan in the Shenandoah Valley, burning barns, killing livestock and pillaging with a free hand so that the Southern Confederacy, if it refused to die in any other way, might die of plain starvation. In a sense, the research that went into these books was simply an effort to find out about the things which the veterans never discussed.

Yet, in an odd way, the old veterans did leave one correct impression: the notion that as young men they had been caught up by something ever so much larger than themselves and that the war in which they fought did settle something for us—or, incredibly, started something which we ourselves have got to finish. It was not only the biggest experience in their own lives; it was in a way the biggest experience in our life as a nation, and it deserves all of the study it is getting.

In any case, these books try to examine a small part of that experience in terms of the men who did the fighting. Those men are all gone now and they have left forever unsaid the things they might have told us, and no one now can speak for them. Here is my attempt to speak about them.

*I*

# John Brown's Body*

## 1969

Anyone who writes about the Civil War is now and then accosted by someone who speaks as follows:

"Isn't there one good book that will give me an understanding of the war—how it happened, why it came out the way it did, and what it all really meant? I don't want a textbook, I don't want a military history, and I don't want a course of required reading; I just want one interesting, readable book that will tell me what the whole business was about. What book should I read?"

The writer's first impulse, of course, is to name five or six of his own books, in practically any order. His next is to suggest that the questioner sit down with the 120 volumes of the Official Records of the War of the Rebellion and see what happens. Then he is tempted to say that the book required simply does not exist. In the end, however, he starts running titles through his mind, looking for the single work that will provide the best understanding of the most moving and important event in American history. I don't know how other people make out with this, but I usually wind up

* Introduction to a special edition of *John Brown's Body* by Stephen Vincent Benét, 1969

by saying: "Read *John Brown's Body* by Stephen Vincent Benét."

In a way this is a surprising sort of conclusion, because Benét's book is neither a history nor a scholarly study of the American people in time of stress. It is a poem—an epic poem, if you please, although it is not much like most epics. It is wholly unpretentious, written in the American idiom, part of it in forthright prose, part of it jingling along as brightly as a squadron of Jeb Stuart's cavalry, part of it as formal and strictly cadenced as a dirge; all of it pulsing with emotion and glowing with the light that comes when a poet's insight touches a moment of inexplicable tragedy. It is solidly based in history, to be sure. Benét says he "tried to cleave to historical fact where such fact was ascertainable." But he found, as everyone does, that some of the facts are missing altogether and that others lie on the page of history indecipherable, conveying a message that is obscured by the shadows of our imperfect knowledge, a message that every man must read for himself. So in the end he examines the Civil War as a poet, not as a historian, and it is as poetry and not as history that his book must be judged.

This is all to the good. The deeper meaning of the American Civil War, for the people who lived through it and for us today, goes beyond the historian's grasp. Here was an event so complex, so deeply based in human emotions, so far-reaching in its final effects, that understanding it is likely to be a matter primarily for the emotions rather than for the cold analysis of facts. It was an experience that was probably felt more deeply than anything else that ever happened to us. We cannot hope to understand it unless we share in that feeling, simply because the depth and intensity of the feeling are among the war's principal legacies. Historians have been interpreting and reinterpreting the struggle for a century, they will go on doing so for a century to come, and much light comes to us that way; but in the end the terrible tragedy calls for the poet's insight simply because it is the poet we have to turn to when we confront the profound impact of tragedy on the human spirit.

Benét wrote *John Brown's Body* a little more than sixty years after the war ended. He was far enough away from it to take a long-range view, but by no means far enough to escape direct involvement: the involvement of the inheritor, if not of the actual participant. Since he wrote this book, more than forty years have passed, so we ourselves have had time not only to reach our own conclusions about the war but to appraise the size and sweep of this work of art that deals with it. We can reach a balanced judgment about the book, if not about the war itself. We have had it for the better part of half a century. How does it read today?

In the first place, *John Brown's Body* stands up. It is as good today as when it was first published. Added knowledge about the war and its leading figures has not turned this book into a literary curiosity. Benét spoke for us as well as for himself. A good deal more is known about the Civil War now than was known in 1928, but what he had to say about it is still valid. The book does not require a series of footnotes pointing out that this, that, or the other aspect of the war looks different now than it looked in his day. It can be taken straight.

It is perfectly true, of course, that the poem is uneven, which is to say that Benét succeeds better in some parts of his task than he does in others. His Lincoln, for example, tends to be a pasteboard figure, and *John Brown's Body* does not add much to our understanding of that unfathomable character. Something of the same is true of his Lee, who remains the marble figure on a pedestal. (Many other men have written about Lee, in the years since Benét wrote; on the whole they have had no better luck than Benét had.) Benét's Grant is another conventional figure, almost a bit player, a brown bear of a man who never steps off the page.

It may be that at least some modern readers will find in
this book a little too much of the swords-and-roses tradition in the treatment of the legendary Southern aristocracy
—the old plantation, the gallant ladies in hoop skirts, the
faithful Negro retainer and the ardent, doomed young men
who rode off to war as to a tournament. A little less vibrato
in the strings, perhaps? No matter. Benét can hardly be
blamed if a century's glorification of the white-pillared tradition has left the theme a little too stylized. Furthermore,
there is this to be said. That tradition, with the reality that
lay back of it, was one of the factors in the situation. It is
one of the things that have to be understood if the war itself
is to be understood. There was a Southern aristocracy, with
a hard pride and an unreal dream and an unreasoned response to an incomprehensible challenge, and it needs just
the kind of attention Benét gave it. Like it or not, this streak
of bright romance was part of the picture.

But the criticisms that can be made are not so important.
Taken as a whole, the book does what it set out to do and
does it very well. And it is both surprising and sobering to
reflect that today's generation may be better placed to
absorb the real inwardness of Benét's message than was his
own generation; because during the last few decades we
have been compelled to see that the issue that ran underneath the Civil War is still very much alive, posing for our
attention what may well be the most urgent and dangerous
of all our problems. What Benét saw clearly—it is the leit-
motif of the whole book, implicit in its most moving and
eloquent passages—is the fact that the Civil War began a
mighty revolutionary process whose end is not yet: the
breaking-forth of the American Negro from the bondage
that kept him from moving up toward everything that we
understand by the noble word Freedom. How can it be
phrased better than Benét put it, when he speaks of the
cataclysm old John Brown helped bring about?

Sometimes there comes a crack in Time itself.
Sometimes the earth is torn by something blind.
Sometimes an image that has stood so long
It seems implanted as the polar star
Is moved against an unfathomed force
That suddenly will not have it any more.

That unfathomed force was on the move in the 1860s, it suddenly would not have chattel slavery any more, and at a fearful cost to everybody it destroyed slavery. But that was only a beginning. We have had a century since then to see to it that the people who escaped from bondage were enabled to go on to full enjoyment of life as free and equal American citizens, and by and large this is a responsibility that we have evaded. We are at last beginning to see that this responsibility cannot be dodged any longer. The evil of second-class citizenship is open, notorious, impossible to ignore, unendurable; and today that unfathomed force that suddenly will not have it any more is on the move again. The warning is clearly visible on every side.

A short time before he became president, Abraham Lincoln made a little speech in Independence Hall, in Philadelphia, in which he remarked that he had "never had a feeling, politically, that did not spring from the sentiments embodied in the Declaration of Independence"—most notably, the statement that all men are created equal. He went on to say that the Declaration gave promise that "in due time the weights would be lifted from the shoulders of all men, and that all should have an equal chance."

A long time has passed since Lincoln made that speech, and the weights have not yet been lifted. We are left with the uneasy knowledge that a crack then was opened in Time itself. What began more than a century ago has not yet ended. We cannot understand what is happening today without understanding what happened in the Civil War. A struggle between the past and the future began then, and it is still going on. More than anything else, we need to see how it began, how it went, and what it finally involves.

So we come back to *John Brown's Body*. This gives us the Genesis. The final Book of Revelation is one to whose writing we must address ourselves.

# Foreword to *Prince Napoleon in America, 1861*[*]

## 1959

Some of the best books on the American Civil War were written by European soldiers, who came to this country either to observe the war at close range or to take actual part in it, and who set down their impressions of a conflict which they found both professionally interesting and strangely unlike the wars of Old World tradition. Fremantle, Ross, Von Borcke, the Comte de Paris—these and others like them wrote books which are still valuable to the student and immensely appealing to the general reader. To the list must now be added this book by Lieutenant-Colonel Camille Ferri Pisani.

Colonel Ferri Pisani came over as aide-de-camp to Prince Napoleon, cousin of Emperor Napoleon III, and he got a good look at America during one of its most crucial periods— the two months immediately following the first battle of Bull Run. He was in a position to see and to hear a good deal. President Lincoln gave a dinner for the Prince and his party, they chatted extensively with Secretary Seward, and both General McClellan and General Beauregard—ardent admirers of the French military tradition, those two—talked

[*] *Prince Napoleon in America, 1861* by Lieutenant-Colonel Camille Ferri Pisani, Indiana University Press, 1959

freely about the war and themselves. The Prince and his
aide saw no actual fighting, but they saw quite a bit of
1861 America—New York and Washington, Pittsburgh and
St. Louis, Boston and Chicago, Niagara Falls and the Great
Lakes; the budding Army of the Potomac and Jeb Stuart's
slashing cavalry, the copper range and the developing nexus
of industrial power, the odd lack of fixed social classes and
the philosophical implications of Massachusetts Unitarian-
ism. All of this the Colonel absorbed, and a great deal of it
he got down on paper. The result: this book, which is good.

Many things about America puzzled the French officer.
Among them was the White House. Here was "a rather nice
palace," obviously fit to be the home of the chief executive;
yet, when the Prince and party called there, there was no
doorman to swing the portal open. The place seemed to be
devoid of lackeys; the Republic, Ferri Pisani mused, ought
either to "give her President enough to live on and to maintain a staff of servants," or put him in a log cabin and be
done with it. Mr. Lincoln seemed awkward and somewhat
embarrassed, and his first meeting with the Prince got down
to a round of handshaking and little more.

The army set-up seemed peculiar, as well. Clearly, Civil
War America was suffering from "the traditional partiality
of democracies for the irregular forces of the State at the
expense of the regular forces"—in plain language, there were
too many volunteers and too many political generals. The
Secretary of War was, obviously, nothing but an administrative officer, a glorified paper-shuffler; command was centered in an aging lieutenant-general (Winfield Scott), whose
functions were for life and irrevocable, and to the Frenchman
this was "a singular anomaly." Ferri Pisani had no way to
see that within a short time the lieutenant-general would
be in retirement, the top command would be vested in
Secretary of War Stanton, who would exercise it to the very
hilt, and the President himself (a well-meaning nonentity,
as the visitors saw him) would actively control and direct

both the Secretary and all of the generals. Observers much closer to the American scene than this French army officer were equally incapable of grasping this point in the summer of 1861.

McClellan talked very freely, and he seems to have left Ferri Pisani with the conviction that "it will not be long before they" (the West Point officers) "will enter the political arena." They were already entering it, as a matter of fact; the Frenchman heard the British Ambassador say, in McClellan's presence, "you are talking with the next President of the United States," and saw McClellan smile modestly in response; what he did not quite foresee was the way in which they would unceremoniously leave the arena when they ran into the unpredictable whimsies of the great American voter. McClellan gave him to understand that the traditional reliance on volunteers and state militia was doomed, and that America would presently come to the formation of a great, permanent army. (In a way, this was a fairly good forecast; however, it was a good ninety years away from even partial fulfillment.)

Northern armies depressed the French regular. Training and discipline were bad, camps were poorly policed and rather dirty, the soldiers seemed spiritless and depressed, and uniforms lacked dash and color. When he got across the line into Virginia, things looked even worse—except that there seemed to be an enthusiasm there that was lacking in the North. The Confederate cavalry looked like no body of horsemen ever seen before—but they had a sparkle and fire, no troopers on earth were as picturesque, as well mounted or as competent in the saddle, and, in fine, "it is undeniable that there is much more passion and ardor among Southern officers than there is in the North."

Beauregard was impressive. Few people have ever given a better one-sentence characterization of this dashing Confederate general: "He does not attempt to restrain his ardent personality, and he is well aware of his reputation." Like many Southerners of the same day, the French were puzzled about the command arrangement in the Confederate army at Manassas—was Joe Johnston over Beauregard, or vice versa? Ferri Pisani could only say: "It is rather difficult to say which of the two exercises the supreme command." As a great favor, Beauregard confided that his original battle plan for Bull Run was modeled on Napoleon's battle plan at Austerlitz: what he failed to mention was that the thing got completely scrambled during the first half-hour of the battle, so that no single part of it went as Beauregard had planned, and in the end the course of events was almost the precise opposite of the original program.

The West Pointers, understandably, fascinated this visitor. Everybody else seemed crude, rough-hewn, lacking in the instincts and background of the gentleman. Each side, however, had generals who had graduated from the military academy and had known each other for many years, and, all in all, "the whole affair seems to be in the hands of friends." This was a good thing, in the eyes of the French regular; to the radical Republicans in Congress it was one of the worst factors in the entire equation, and men like McClellan and Fitz-John Porter were presently retired to the side lines because of it. The radicals saw what the visitor could not see: that the whole affair was not, and could never be, "in the hands of friends"—something fundamental was at stake, the affair was in the hands of sworn enemies, and all the niceties of well-bred behavior would go out of the window in the face of the urgencies propounded by men like Sherman, Sheridan, and Bedford Forrest. Ferri Pisani believed that public sentiment was turning to men who were opposed "to any moral or material disorder," but moral and material disorder were presently to become the order of the day. There were things about the American Civil War that no regular army man fresh from Europe could be expected to grasp in a two-months visit.

Ferri Pisani grasped a good deal, however, and throughout he was a faithful and ingratiating reporter. Whether he was writing about Pennsylvania's model penitentiary, American trains, steamboats on the Great Lakes, or the farmers of Illinois, he preserved for today's readers a clear picture of what America was like when the Civil War was just beginning to exert its profound influence. He went by boat from Lake Erie clear up to Lake Superior's copper country, and he left a sketch of the trip that will make any nostalgic American wish that he himself could have been along. Some of his notes are more striking than he could have realized. Far away in the Upper Peninsula of Michigan, he met a bearded captain of army engineers who had been isolated there for a long time on survey duty, and who was delighted because he had at last been ordered to Washington to take part in the new war: George Gordon Meade, who two years later was to be the victor at Gettysburg.

Secretary of State Seward took the visitor in, a little, as he was likely to do to anybody. From him, apparently, Ferri Pisani received the impression that the real leader of the Republican party and the real power in the government was Seward himself; Lincoln was a minor character, brought to the top largely by Seward's own machinations—a long, lanky man "close to the Celtic type of the Auvergne region," worthy enough, "an honest and very dedicated man, but without brilliance." It was Seward, however, who, if really dangerous times came, would display the suppleness and brilliance needed to save the Republic.

Well, closer observers than this French officer missed the same boat, and Ferri Pisani did pretty well, all things considered. He missed a few things, as any man would have been bound to miss them in the summer of 1861. He knew about Johnston and Beauregard, but not about Robert E. Lee; he wrote of McClellan and McDowell, but he had never heard (as no one else had heard, then) of U. S. Grant and William Tecumseh Sherman; but he saw the profound contradictions in the United States Congress of that day, when

forthright Southerners like John Breckenridge still sat in
the Senate, and when no man, glancing about either House,
could be quite certain that the legislator he was looking at
was not in favor of disruption of the Union. And if he believed that professional soldiers would eventually rise above
sectional discord and take control of the war, men like Mc-
Clellan, who could have been expected to know better, believed the same thing.

What Ferri Pisani did do was present a straight, as-of-the-
moment view of America at the brief hour when the future
had not quite begun to take shape. If he committed himself
to faulty appraisals, the important thing about them is
that they were precisely the appraisals which any intelligent,
well-informed outsider at that moment would have been
bound to make: that is, they were forecasts which were solidly based on the appearances of things in the summer of
1861. What neither this visitor nor most Americans of that
day could realize was that something entirely new was beginning to happen. The past was no guide, but it was all the
guide there was just then, and Ferri Pisani faithfully followed it.

In any case, what we get here is a moving, colorful, and
spirited account of what a French army officer saw in
America during two of the most critical months of its history. It is very much worth reading, it contains sidelights
of historical importance, and from first to last it is extremely
interesting and enjoyable. Our Civil War literature is richer
for the publication of these memoirs.

# President Lincoln and General McClellan*
## 1960

The military experience which Abraham Lincoln brought to the Presidency was very sketchy. He had been captain of volunteers in the Black Hawk War, and years later he made a little speech in Congress poking fun at his brief and inglorious career as a soldier. He had had no combat service. It is said that he once was ordered to carry a wooden sword for two days as penalty for his inability to maintain discipline over his rowdy frontiersmen. Once when an old Potawatomi Indian wandered into camp Lincoln kept his men from lynching the poor creature only by taking off his coat and offering to thrash each man personally, one at a time.

That was the extent of Lincoln's military background. Then, for four years beginning in the spring of 1861, Lincoln found himself Commander-in-chief of the nation's armed forces in the nation's most searching war.

During the all-important formative period of this war, from July 1861 to November 1862, Lincoln's principal lieutenant was Major General George B. McClellan. A brilliant young West Point graduate, McClellan had fought with distinction in the Mexican War. He had gone to the Crimea as

* *Lincoln for the Ages*, edited by Ralph G. Newman, Doubleday & Company, Inc., 1960

official War Department observer to report on the way European armies were handled in the field. He was, in short, a soldier with solid professional training and experience, possessed of vast administrative ability and a high degree of personal magnetism.

The contrast between President and General could not have been more striking. McClellan knew all the things about war that Lincoln did not know, with one significant exception. He never quite understood what the American Civil War was all about or how it had to be won. Lincoln did. So, in the end, it was Lincoln who saved the Union and McClellan who went down in history as a gifted and devoted soldier who somehow did not quite measure up.

For a time the two made a good team. An expert organizer, McClellan took the formless mass of raw recruits who were pouring into Washington after the Bull Run disaster and created the superb Army of the Potomac. He trained that army, organized and equipped it, and infused it with magnificent morale—a belief in itself that endured through four years of terrible fighting. Long after he himself had left the service the veterans spoke of themselves as McClellan's men. For no other soldier did they have the intense personal loyalty they had for McClellan.

But McClellan was also gravely handicapped. He was excessively cautious, and his caution kept him from realizing that the great function of a Federal troop commander was to take the North's immense advantage in muscle and apply it inexorably against the weaker Confederates. He was always convinced that he was outnumbered, and this strange delusion kept him from waging war in the remorseless, unceasing way of a Grant or a Sherman.

Nor was McClellan ever able to see that this war was not going according to the traditional European pattern. Traditionally two nations which went to war followed certain rules. They did not make war on civilians; war was strictly a matter for soldiers. They campaigned, fought, maneuvered, seized strategic points—and sooner or later one side would find itself at a ruinous disadvantage and would sue for peace. Then some sort of treaty would be worked out and the war would end.

But there could be no treaty to end this war. It had to go to a finish. The South wanted absolute independence and it would agree to nothing less, and until it was made literally incapable of fighting any longer the war would go on. This meant that the war would be very grim and merciless. It was not enough for the Federals to defeat opposing armies; they had to destroy them, and to destroy also the economic and political foundation which supported them. They had, for instance, to dismantle the institution of human slavery, not because they necessarily had anything against slavery but simply because slavery made it possible for the Confederate armies to go on fighting. On the surface the whole thing looked like a regular war, but in fact it was a civil war, which meant that the traditional military rules were of very little use.

Of all the men in the North, Abraham Lincoln was the one who understood this the most clearly. From the beginning he treated the conflict as a revolutionary situation and used revolutionary means to fight it. Like Clausewitz he saw war as an extension of politics, and he played politics vigorously. He made generals out of political leaders, not because he supposed that they knew anything about military affairs but because he wanted to bring to the Northern war effort the political support which these leaders could command. He let his attitude toward slavery be governed by the political necessities of the moment; until the Northern attitude hardened he refused to let emancipation be made government policy, but once the political atmosphere changed he had no hesitation in issuing the Emancipation Proclamation, even though he had to stretch his legal authority to or beyond the breaking point in order to do it. Quite simply he was out to destroy the Southern Confederacy in any way possible, using any implement that came to his hand.

All of this meant that the President and the General were forever cut off from a complete meeting of minds. McClellan, always moving slowly and cautiously, insisting on treating this as another war in the established military pattern, was bound to seem—to ardent patriots in the Administration, at least—as a man of lukewarm loyalties. When he took his army down to the Virginia peninsula in the spring of 1862 and lost first the initiative and then the campaign to the hard-hitting Robert E. Lee, leaders in Congress and in the Cabinet muttered that he did not really want to win. McClellan's army was pulled back to Washington and most of his troops were entrusted to the inexpert General John Pope, who led them to a crushing defeat at the second battle of Bull Run. Over the violent objection of most of his advisors Lincoln restored McClellan to the command, knowing that only he could pull the dejected army together again. McClellan performed this task expertly, and when Lee crossed the Potomac to invade the North McClellan followed, brought him to battle at Antietam Creek, beat him, and sent him back into Virginia. Then, with all of the advantage on his side, McClellan refused to conduct a vigorous pursuit. As a matter of fact he made no pursuit at all for some weeks, and Lee was granted the breathing space he needed so desperately to reorganize and re-equip his shattered army. In the end Lincoln finally lost patience and removed McClellan from command. As a soldier McClellan's career ended in November 1862.

Ironically enough the one victory McClellan won—the tremendous battle of Antietam—accomplished precisely what McClellan himself did not want accomplished. It changed the pattern of the whole war, turning it unmistakably into the kind of war which McClellan did not approve. For it was the victory at Antietam which persuaded Lincoln to issue the Emancipation Proclamation. From that moment on the North was fighting not merely for reunion but also for the abolition of slavery. If before this there had ever been a chance that the war might someday end in a compromise, with a restored Union and ample guarantee for Southern rights, that chance was gone after Antietam. Now the last chance for compromise was ruled out. The war could end only in Southern independence or in total destruction of the Confederacy *and* of the social, political, and economic framework which characterized Southern society as a whole.

McClellan's removal, in short, was inevitable after Antietam. Whether he himself realized the fact or not McClellan by this time had become the representative of the substantial number of people in the North who wanted the Union restored but did not want the South wrecked in the process; the Northerners who saw no reason why they should interfere with slavery and who detested the abolitionists nearly as heartily as did the Southerners themselves. McClellan embodied that point of view, and his great victory left him with no place to stand.

Up to this point the relationship between Lincoln and McClellan had been basically that of two men who in spite of friction are working together for the same end. McClellan would have been driven out of the Army much earlier if he had not had Lincoln's support; without Lincoln he assuredly would not have been restored to command for the Antietam campaign. In turn he had not served Lincoln too badly. He had created a magnificent army and he had done some good things with it. If Antietam was in many ways the decisive battle of the entire war McClellan has to be recorded as the general who won it.

But before the war ended the two appeared as open antagonists. In the late summer of 1864 the Democratic party nominated McClellan as its candidate for the Presidency. McClellan himself had no notion of stopping the war before reunion had been won, but many of his supporters had other ideas, and Lincoln himself believed that if McClellan won the election he would do so on terms which would make it impossible for him to overthrow the Confederacy. Justly or otherwise the election came to be regarded as the decisive test of the Northern electorate's willingness to carry the war to a victorious conclusion. Lincoln won, and McClellan went off to join the shadows.

Of the two men—co-workers, first, and then opponents —it was obviously Lincoln who had the broader concept of things. He understood McClellan and he understood the war; McClellan understood Lincoln very imperfectly and understood the war little better, nor did he like what he understood of either. But although he goes down in history simply as one of the men whom Lincoln used and then discarded he had his own place in the story of the struggle. He created the Army of the Potomac and gave it the character that carried it through the war, and he left in the hearts of his soldiers an image which the passing years never dimmed. To the end of their lives the veterans of that army had a special place in their affections for George B. McClellan. They were not impressionable men; the man who won and kept that place in their emotions had a quality whose distinctive essence should not be dimmed by the fact that the President he served was incomparably the greater man of the two.

# Introduction to *The Battle of Gettysburg** 

## 1957

One of the genuine classics of Civil War literature is Frank
Haskell's account of the Battle of Gettysburg. It has been
used by students of the war for more than half a century,
but it has never quite reached the general reader; which
is a pity, for it speaks to everyone and not just to the historian. Now, at last, it is being made available to all.

It is valuable in two ways. First of all, this Union officer
was on the staff of the divisional commander who held the
precise part of the Federal line against which was directed
the most famous military assault in American history, Pickett's Charge. During all of it, Haskell was in the exact storm
center; and in this account, with the heat of battle still on
him—he wrote the manuscript within two weeks of the
battle itself—he tells just what happened there, under the
battle smoke that must always dim the sight of later generations. It is hardly going too far to say that no one can write
a full account of Gettysburg without consulting Haskell.

In the second place, Haskell could write. He could over-
write, as a matter of fact, and in places his prose gets
altogether too purple for modern taste; but he did have the

* By Frank A. Haskell, Houghton Mifflin, 1957

talent to convey the look and the sound and the feel of what he had been through, and he does give his reader an emotional understanding of that tremendous fight and of the effect it had on the men who were in it. Any visitor to the stone wall and the famous clump of trees on Cemetery Ridge is bound to find himself musing, as he stands on that historic ground: What was it really like up here then? As far as the question can ever be answered for one who was not there, Haskell answers it.

Haskell's own military career was brief but distinguished. Born in Vermont in 1828, he was graduated from Dartmouth College in the class of 1854, and in the fall of that year he went to Madison, Wisconsin, and entered the practice of law. When the Civil War came he promptly enlisted, and on June 20, 1861, he was commissioned first lieutenant in Company I of the 6th Wisconsin Infantry. This regiment was presently sent east, with Haskell serving as regimental adjutant, and in the spring of 1862, along with the 2nd and 7th Wisconsin and the 19th Indiana regiments (to which, a few months later, was added the 24th Michigan) it became a part of what was to be one of the most famous combat units in the Army of the Potomac, the celebrated "Iron Brigade."

This brigade was commanded by Brigadier General John Gibbon, a tough, capable West Pointer in his mid-thirties, who promptly made Haskell an aid on his staff. The two served with the brigade in the battles of Second Bull Run, South Mountain and Antietam, and in the fall of 1862, when Gibbon was raised to divisional command, he saw to it that Haskell remained on his staff. Haskell stayed with him through Fredericksburg, Chancellorsville and Gettysburg, and won both Gibbon's professional admiration and personal affection. In his report on Gettysburg, Gibbon wrote that Haskell had distinguished himself in every battle "by his conspicuous coolness and bravery," and added: "It has always been a source of regret to me that our military system offers no plan for rewarding his merit and services as they deserve."

There is plenty of evidence of Haskell's daring and leadership at Gettysburg. Major General Winfield Scott Hancock, doughty commander of the Second Corps, praised him in his report of the battle. So did two of his brigade commanders, Brigadier General William Harrow and Colonel Norman J. Hall; and Gibbon, long afterward, wrote: "I have always thought that to him, more than to any one man, are we indebted for the repulse of Lee's assault. His personal gallantry in aiding the officers in re-forming their overpowered troops was seen and commented upon by many, whilst his quick judgment in using his authority as a staff officer of his absent general in moving assistance to the critical point was admirable."

Gibbon was badly wounded at Gettysburg, and so was Hancock, and for a time after the battle the Second Corps was under the leadership of Brigadier General William Hays (who is not to be confused with Brigadier General Alexander Hays, the able leader of one of the Second Corps divisions). Haskell served on William Hays's staff for a time, and the experience seems not to have been a happy one. Hays proved so inept an infantry commander that he was presently replaced by Major General G. K. Warren, who served until Hancock returned to duty. A fellow staff officer left an amusing picture of Haskell's lot during the Hays regime. Hays liked a morning drink of whisky, but refused to let himself touch the stuff before ten o'clock. Regularly, half an hour or thereabouts before the appointed time (says this staff officer), the general would stick his head out of his tent, look anxiously at the sun, and call out: "What time is it, Mr. Haskell?" From Haskell would come the matter-of-fact reply: "Nine-thirty, sir." The general would look about for a moment and then would say: "Suppose we call it ten, Mr. Haskell."

It was during this period that Haskell wrote his account

of the Battle of Gettysburg. He did not specifically write
it for publication, although it is possible to guess that the
idea that it would someday see print was never far from
his mind. He sent it to his brother, H. M. Haskell, of Portage,
Wisconsin, who offered it to the editor of the local weekly
paper; the editor, finding it far too long for his limited space,
was unable to use it, and the article was not printed until
long after Haskell's death.

In any case, Haskell got the reward Gibbon was talking
about before either Gibbon or Hancock returned to duty.
In February, 1864, he was named colonel of the new 36th
Wisconsin Infantry. He hurried to Madison to help organize
the regiment and prepare it for service, and brought it
east early in May, just after the Army of the Potomac had
begun the grinding, costly campaign that would take it
from the Wilderness through Spotsylvania and Cold Harbor
to Petersburg.

Haskell never did see Petersburg. His regiment—a unit
in the First Brigade of Gibbon's division—had reached the
army too late to take part in the earlier battles, but by the
first of June it was ready and on June 3, when Gibbon's
division was one of the organizations assigned to the fearful assault at Cold Harbor, the First Brigade led one of his
columns of attack, with the 36th Wisconsin in the front
line.

Cold Harbor was the never-forgotten black day in the
history of the army. On June 3, attacking Lee along a
broad front, the Army of the Potomac lost something like
7000 men in half an hour without gaining the slightest
advantage. The commander of Gibbon's First Brigade was
killed just as the attack got under way, and Haskell took
over the brigade leadership and tried to continue the advance against a murderous storm of rifle fire. The attempt
was hopeless, and Haskell ordered his men to lie down.
An officer in the 36th Wisconsin wrote afterward that
Haskell's role here was the precise reverse of his role at

Gettysburg. At Gettysburg, he had been helping to defend an impregnable position against a doomed attack; here he was leading a similarly doomed attack against a position equally impregnable, and he lost his life in the process. Unable to go forward, he was standing erect on the firing line, looking to right and left to make sure that his men were taking cover, and he got a bullet through the brain and fell lifeless. Informed of his death, Gibbon cried: "My God! I have lost my best friend, and one of the best soldiers in the Army of the Potomac has fallen!"

So that was Haskell's military career—distinguished, active, ending in tragedy. If it were not for the little memoir he wrote, he would be remembered dimly, only as one of the surprisingly large number of young men who came out of civil life in the 1860s to display an extraordinary talent for soldiering. All Civil War armies had them, North and South alike, and the war could not have been fought without them. None of the Civil War volunteer units had what a modern soldier would consider adequate training; it used to be an axiom that volunteer soldiers would go just as far, on the battlefield, as their officers would take them. Officers like Haskell would take them quite a distance.

Haskell's narrative of Gettysburg never got widespread public attention. Some fifteen years after it had been written his brother had it printed in pamphlet form, for private distribution. In 1898 it was reprinted as part of the history of the Class of 1854, Dartmouth College. In this version, it was edited down rather substantially, and much of the material in Haskell's account which reflected on the conduct of the Eleventh Army Corps, and on Major General Daniel Sickles, was eliminated. This version was reprinted in 1908 by the Commandery of Massachusetts, Military Order of the Loyal Legion of the United States; and the full, unabridged version was printed shortly thereafter under the auspices of the Wisconsin History Commission, in an edition of 2500 copies. It was also printed in Vol. 43 of the Harvard

Classics, in 1910, and in 1937 a limited edition was published by the *Titusville Herald,* at Titusville, Pa. It quickly became a standard reference work for students of the battle —it is this text which is reprinted herewith—but the general reader rarely saw it.

Come to think of it, that statement probably needs modification. Some general readers did see it, most notably a number of aging men who had themselves fought at Gettysburg as members of the famous Philadelphia Brigade, a Second Corps unit led by Brigadier General Alexander Webb. They saw it and promptly became furious. Webb's brigade had held the angle in the stone wall at Gettysburg and took the first shock of Pickett's charge, and in his narrative Haskell asserts that the brigade broke and ran and that he rode among the fugitives, swinging with the flat of his sword and calling on all cowards to return to duty. The association of Philadelphia Brigade survivors met, appointed a committee to look into the matter, and in 1910 issued a pamphlet in indignant rebuttal. Admitting that Haskell's record as a soldier was very good, the pamphlet insisted that "as a writer of events of the war he was absurd, reckless and unreliable" and it called on everyone who had given the pamphlet publication to recant and do justice to brave soldiers.

Justice and recantation the brigade could not get. The secretary and editor of the Wisconsin History Commission, Reuben G. Thwaites, wrote to a committee of the brigade that if the Haskell account was worth reprinting at all— and, he added, it seemed to the Commission that it was very much worth it—"the only course open to us, as historians, was to present it just as it was originally issued"; to modify it in any way would be to ruin it as historical material. Old General Webb himself, still alive at that time, wrote his former comrades that "what Haskell wrote, he wrote in ignorance," and urged them to let their denial of his assertions be "strong and yet courteous." A close friend of Haskell wrote that he had talked with Haskell several times, after Gettysburg, and asserted that he had "good reason for stating that had Haskell lived until the close of the war the criticisms contained in his diary would not have been made public." With all of this—and with publication of their own spirited pamphlet—the Philadelphians had to rest content.

That Haskell somewhat overstated the extent of the rout in Webb's brigade seems quite likely. Part of the brigade unquestionably did withdraw when Pickett's men came rolling in over the wall, but Gibbon probably put the case more accurately; the men were overpowered, rather than routed. They re-formed and fought to the end of the battle, they suffered heavy casualties, and when the dust had settled they had a fine haul of prisoners of war and captured battle flags to show for their trouble. Haskell, to repeat, wrote when his emotions were still at white heat—he began to write his manuscript on July 14, less than a fortnight after the battle had ended—and he was trying to present a stirring and graphic account of the most stupendous experience in his life. If he did something less than full justice to the men of Webb's brigade, it is not entirely a matter for surprise.

Of the general value of his narrative as a historic document there is no question. He wrote from imperfect knowledge and without benefit of the long backward glance, and a good many minor flaws can be detected; but as a picture of what things were like on Cemetery Ridge during the turmoil of the war's climactic battle his account does stand up. This testimony comes from a spot directly under the guns, and part of its value lies in the fact that the author never had the chance to recast it in the light of postwar knowledge and reflection. What he saw, felt and experienced he put down on paper; he had been in a position to see, feel and experience the worst that any battle could do, and the high readability of his manuscript comes from that very fact.

It must be emphasized that this whole book is the product of the middle of the stormy summer of 1863. In what he had to say Haskell reflects the unvarnished feelings of a Union army officer writing at a time when the outcome of the war still hung in the balance. The Confederate soldier, to him, was still "the Rebel," former U. S. Army officers who fought on the Southern side were simply traitors, and if their valor had to be respected—and Haskell respected it, up to the hilt—their motives (as Haskell appraised them) did not. Haskell was in no mood to deal judiciously with all of the tragic lights and shadows of the Lost Cause; when he was writing, it had by no means become lost, and on the day of his death it looked very much as if it might eventually become victorious.

So here it is: one of the great, almost unknown books to come out of the Civil War, violently partisan, unrevised, infused with all of the fury of combat. The separate chapters in the great story of Gettysburg are almost innumerable; here is one of the best, a chapter which has the power to put the reader back in the middle of a fight that ended nearly a century ago. As Haskell himself wrote: "It is not designed to be a history, but simply *my account* of the battle."

He went on to remark, very truly, that a full account of Gettysburg as it actually was "will never, can never, be made." It could not be done by the participants themselves; each man was overwhelmed by the part he himself had seen. It cannot be done by members of a later generation, because they never saw any of it. As Haskell himself said:

"By-and-by, out of the chaos of trash and falsehood that the newspapers hold, out of the disjointed mass of reports, out of the traditions and tales that come down from the field, some eye that never saw the battle will select, and some pen will write, what will be named *the history*. With that the world will be and, if we are alive, we must be, content."

All of us who undertake to write about Gettysburg need to read Haskell's book. Most particularly, I think, we need to read the paragraph just quoted. It tends to induce a much-needed humility.

But in the long run this book is for the general reader rather than for the specialist. It offers an understanding and an emotional experience that can be had from few other Civil War books. It is very, very much worth reading.

# The Generalship of Ulysses S. Grant*

## 1964

The American Civil War confronted the professional soldier with a vexing series of problems which went far beyond anything he could possibly have been expected to learn at West Point.

West Point gave its graduates a first-rate training, but it told them very little about some of the things that would be required of them in the 1860s. It had trained them for a different sort of war altogether—for a war of professionals, with set rules, established values and recognized limits— and the very fact that it had trained them well and thoroughly meant that they were apt to find themselves bewildered once the nation thrust them into a war which made up its own rules as it went along, groped blindly toward values which had never been defined, and came in the end to recognize no limits whatsoever.

For the Civil War resembled war as set forth in the textbooks only to an extent. It was, to begin with, what its traditional name says it was—a civil war, not a war with some foreign nation—and it contained elements West Point had never dreamed of. It had to be fought by citizen-

* *Grant, Lee, Lincoln and the Radicals*, edited by Grady McWhiney, Northwestern University Press, 1964

soldiers drawn from a land which might be exceedingly
pugnacious but which had an immense impatience with
restraints and formalities. Problems of politics and of eco-
nomics were woven through every part of its fabric. The
techniques of a newly mechanized age had to be taken into
account. On top of everything, it was on both sides a war of
the people, whose imperious and often impatient desires
exerted a constant pressure which no general could ignore.

To appraise the generalship of any of the great soldiers
in that war, therefore, it is necessary to understand first just
what it was that the Civil War required of them. It required straight military competence, to be sure, and those
indefinable qualities of leadership which professional training may develop but cannot implant; but it also called for
a great adaptability, a readiness to find unorthodox solu-
tions for unorthodox problems, an understanding of just
what it was that the American people were trying to do in
that terrible war they were waging with themselves.

Now the first thing to take into consideration here is that
the American Civil War was—or became, not long after it
had begun—an all-out war; which means that it was essentially quite unlike the kind of war professional soldiers
of the mid-nineteenth century usually had in mind.

Each side was fighting for an absolute; to compromise
was to lose. The South was fighting for independence, the
North for reunion. Inextricably interwoven with these opposing causes was the matter of chattel slavery. The men of
each side, in other words, came at an early stage to believe
passionately that they were fighting both for national survival and for human freedom—the Southerner, for his own
personal freedom, the Northerner, for freedom in the abstract, but both for freedom. Each side, accordingly, believed
that it was fighting for a high and holy cause and that final
victory was worth any conceivable sacrifice. Victory was
more important than anything else. What it cost did not
matter, and what it would finally mean could be settled

later on; while the war lasted victory would be pursued with immense singleness of purpose. And to drive for absolute victory is of course to wage all-out war in the modern manner.[1]

Now this was not what most professional soldiers of that era had in mind at all. They had been brought up in a doctrine that came down from the eighteenth century. Wars were usually fought for limited objectives, and they were fought in a limited way; they were primarily matters for the armies, and they were conducted up to the point where they began to cost more than they were likely to be worth, at which point they were brought to an end. The settlement that finally ended a war was of course a matter for governments to determine, not for generals; what the generals had to remember was that sooner or later there would be some sort of settlement, and that until the settlement was made it was wise to conduct affairs without causing too much breakage.

This meant that wars had to a certain extent become formalized. They were in a way like immense chess games, performed with intricate maneuvers that followed the book; going by the book, a good general always knew when he was licked, and behaved accordingly. One of the most cerebral and highly educated of Northern soldiers, General Don Carlos Buell, told the court of inquiry which considered his case after he had been removed from the command of the Army of the Cumberland that it ought to be quite possible to conduct an entire campaign successfully without fighting a single battle.[2] Make the right moves and you will win: you do not need to be especially combative, but you must be very careful, leaving as little as possible to chance, never moving until everything is ready, making those maneuvers and occupying those strategic points which will finally persuade your opponent that he has been beaten.

This attitude formed part of the mental background of a

great many of the professional soldiers who were given important assignments in the early part of the Civil War, and it was precisely this attitude which kept some of them from being successful. This, to repeat, was a different kind of war. The two sides which were involved were not going to quit until somebody made them quit. Victories would go, not to the man who followed the book faithfully, but to the man who was willing and able to get in close and slug until something broke. He would, to be sure, need a good deal of professional ability to get in close and to slug effectively after he got there, but his ultimate objective was, quite simply, the enemy's will and ability to resist. Until he broke that he accomplished nothing.

This requirement rested with particular weight on the Federal generals. The Southerner had one thing working for him: it was always conceivable that even if he did not actually win he could compel the Northerner to give up the fight from sheer war weariness. The Northerner had no similar reliance. He would get no final victory unless Confederate strength was utterly destroyed. He had to be aggressive, because a stalemate would work in favor of his opponent. Whether he realized the fact or not, the Federal soldier was fighting to enforce an unconditional surrender. It was his task, not merely to compel his foe to come to terms, but to obliterate a nation.

It was not easy for the average professional soldier to grasp this point, and a number of good men never got an inkling of it. It is perhaps significant that the three Federal generals who most often were called "brilliant" by their Old Army associates—Buell, McClellan, and Halleck—were men who failed utterly to see this requirement and who accordingly never measured up to the high expectations which had been made regarding them. These men had studied the science of war with great care, and they brought keen intelligence to the task. Their trouble was that the Civil War called on them for qualities which their studies had never revealed to them. In his statement that it should be possible to win a campaign without actually fighting a battle, Buell was entirely correct—by the book. But the book did not apply in his case, because his assignment in Kentucky and Tennessee could not be discharged as long as the Confederate Army of Tennessee remained in existence. It was not enough for him to put it at a disadvantage. He had to take it apart, and he could not conceivably do that without compelling it to fight until it could fight no more.

In the same way, Halleck completely missed his opportunity after the battle of Shiloh and the fall of Corinth in the spring of 1862. He had assembled an army of perhaps 125,000 men in northern Mississippi, and to oppose him Beauregard had substantially fewer than half that many men. With the light of after-knowledge it is easy to see that Halleck ought to have pressed his advantage to the utmost, driving his foe on relentlessly and compelling him at last to fight a battle that could only result in annihilation. Instead, Halleck went by the book. He undertook to occupy territory, dividing his army into detachments, leisurely setting to work to consolidate his advantages; he saw the map, and the things which a strategist ought to do on it, rather than the men in arms who carried the opposing nation on the points of their bayonets. Behaving thus, he gave the Confederacy a breathing spell in which it assembled new levies, dug in to resist a new Federal offensive, and in the end took the initiative away from him and marched north almost to the Ohio River. The war went on for two more years.

Another responsibility rested on men in the Federal high command. The Federal government has almost overwhelming advantages in the Civil War, from the beginning to the end. In manpower, in money, in raw materials and manufacturing capacity, in access to world markets, in the ability to raise, feed, equip, and transport armies—in all of the things that go to make up military capacity in time of war

—the resources of the North so far overshadowed those of the South that one is compelled at times to wonder what ever made the leaders of the Confederacy think that they could possibly win. This enormous advantage was bound to bring victory, in the end, if it could just be applied steadily, remorselessly and without a break, and it was above all other things up to the Federal generals to see this and to govern themselves accordingly. They had, in other words, the ability to apply and maintain a pressure which the Confederacy could not hope to resist. They could afford mistakes, they could afford wastage, they could afford almost anything except the failure to make constant use of the power that was available to them.

It was just here, perhaps, that the reality of the Civil War departed most completely from the orthodox military tradition. Two very different economic and social systems were struggling for survival. One of them was fitted to win such a struggle if it went to the limit, and the other, the weaker system, was not. In effect, a Confederate leader had his own army to rely on and nothing more; the Federal leader had not only his own army but the infinite war-potential of a rich, populous, highly organized industrial state. "Brilliance" in the purely military field was the reliance of the Southern soldier—possibly his only reliance—as Robert E. Lee abundantly demonstrated; the Northerner's reliance was something quite different, calling not so much for an understanding of the rules of war as for an understanding of the ways by which a great nation enforces its will.

Along with everything else this required the Northern general to give a certain amount of thought to the institution of chattel slavery, simply because the slave system was one of the main props—perhaps the most important one of all—for the Southern economy which was the ultimate support of Southern armies. This prop, while important, was exceedingly fragile. One of the facts that had driven slave-state leaders to secession in the first place had been the dawning realization that the peculiar institution could continue to exist only if it were carefully protected against all outside interference. A general who took a hostile army into slave territory was providing such interference, whether he meant to or not. Regardless of his own feelings in respect to slavery, the peculiar institution became of necessity one of his military objectives. He was fighting, to repeat, a total war, and in a total war the enemy's economy is to be undermined in any way possible. Slavery was the southern economy's most vulnerable spot, and a Northern general could not be neutral in respect to it. Every time one of his soldiers extracted a plantation hand from bondage—every time the mere presence of his army disorganized the slave-labor system in its area and caused a blind exodus of men and women from the huddled slave cabins—he was helping to disarm the Confederacy.

It must be confessed that the Northern general was under certain handicaps during the first year and one-half of the struggle. Up to the fall of 1862, it was official government policy that the war was being fought solely to restore the Union, and generals were instructed not to campaign against slavery. This, to be sure, was a vain hope, but generals were supposed to follow top policy even when it was impossible; and this policy could not be followed, simply because the private soldiers took things into their own hands. The soldiers quickly came to equate the possession of slaves with opposition to the Union. In places like Kentucky this often led them to despoil the property of men who were stoutly Unionist in their leanings, but there was no help for it. Regardless of what the generals might say, the private Federal soldier was predominantly an emancipationist whenever he got south, not because he himself had any especial feelings against slavery but simply because he realized that slavery supported the nation he was fighting against.

Slavery, indeed, was the one institution which could not

possibly survive an all-out war. A Union general might deplore this fact, but he was obliged to take it into account. Here, in short, was one more extremely important field in which the professional soldier's training and traditions were of no use to him. He had to understand what made his country tick, and in the long run what he did had to be done in the light of that understanding. There was nothing in the textbooks to help him. Like the men he commanded, the general had to have a good deal of the citizen-soldier in him.

It is sometimes said, indeed, that the most successful generals in the Civil War were men who had left the army in the prewar years and had had experience in the civilian world. This is only partly true. It applies to such men as Grant and Sherman, to be sure, but it does not apply at all to men like Lee, Joseph E. Johnston, Stonewall Jackson, and George Thomas, who had never been or wanted to be anything but professional soldiers; and one of the men who most faithfully tried to make war by the old tradition was a man who had left the army and had had a highly successful career in business—George B. McClellan. Yet one is bound to feel that particularly on the Northern side a man who had had some experience outside of the army might have gained something from it. The war had strong non-professional aspects, and an officer who had something of a non-professional viewpoint—who had learned, by first-hand experience, something about the way the American people go about their business and try to make their will felt—could derive an advantage from that fact.

I suggest that it is only against this background that we can intelligently evaluate the generalship of the man under whom the Federal armies finally won the Civil War—Ulysses S. Grant.

Grant first comes on the wartime stage in the fall of 1861, at Cairo, Illinois, where he commanded a body of troops which would presently be used in the attempt to open the

Mississippi Valley. It is possible to see, even before this first campaign got under way, some of his essential qualities: an uncomplicated belief in direct action, a realization of the things that could be done with raw troops, and a constant desire to strike for complete victory rather than for the attainment of a minor advantage.

In September, 1861, Grant commanded approximately 15,000 men. All of his men—like all of the other men in Union and Confederate armies at that time—were poorly trained and poorly armed, but he wanted to use them at once. He told his chief of staff, John A. Rawlins, that when two unprepared armies faced one another, the commander of one of those armies would gain very little by waiting until his troops were thoroughly prepared. This, said Grant, simply meant that his opponent would have time to do the same thing, and in the end the relative strengths of the opposing armies would be about what they had been at the start.[3] It might be noted that in expressing this opinion Grant was departing from military orthodoxy. The professional soldier had a natural distaste for trying to make a campaign with an army whose training, discipline, and equipment were deficient, and the shambling assemblages of newly uniformed young men who made up the armies in the fall of 1861 had deficiencies too obvious to overlook. The disaster at Bull Run simply underlined the point. In his ability to see that the other side was equally handicapped, Grant was being definitely unprofessional. His attitude here was much more the attitude of the civilian than of the trained soldier; he was quite willing to use an imperfect instrument, provided that his opponent's instrument was equally imperfect.

And so Grant, that fall, wanted to attack the Confederate stronghold at Columbus, on the Mississippi River. He knew that his troops were by no means ready to confront a trained, tightly organized army, but he knew also that they were not going to have to confront anything of the kind. The army they would fight was in no better shape than themselves. Under the circumstances, Grant wanted to fight as soon as possible.

There is of course another side to this argument, and Grant doubtless got a certain amount of enlightenment from his first battle, the sharp engagement fought at Belmont, across the river from Columbus. Here Grant attacked a Confederate force and drove it from the field in temporary rout, which was just what he had expected to do. What he had not anticipated was the fact that his unready troops fell into complete disorder because they had won a victory. They got out of hand, wandered about looting the Confederate camp, listening to spread-eagle speeches by their colonels, and in general acting as if the battle was over. The Confederates across the river sent over fresh troops, and Grant's men in turn were driven off in rout, escaping final disaster only because Grant managed at last to get them back to their transports and take them up the river to safety. Because they were so imperfectly disciplined and organized, they had lost a victory which they had won.[4]

Grant's original idea, in other words, needed to be toned down slightly. But it did have some merit, and it went hand in hand with another notion, equally repugnant to military orthodoxy. Not long after Belmont, it was suggested to Grant that by proper maneuvering he could compel the Confederates to evacuate that stronghold at Columbus. Grant dissented vigorously. There was (he insisted) very little point in merely compelling the enemy's army to retreat; sooner or later that army would have to be fought, when it was fought it would have to be destroyed outright —dispersed in open combat, or hemmed in and captured lock, stock, and barrel—and this might as well be done at once.[5] Making the enemy retreat simply postponed the showdown that had to come eventually.

The big business, in short, was to fight, to fight all-out, and to win the most decisive victory imaginable. There was no point in a campaign for limited objectives. Any battle which left the opposing army on its feet and breathing struck General Grant as imperfect.

It is a little surprising to find a Federal general feeling this way in the fall of 1861. The war then was still young, and the Northern government was still trying, with much fumbling and inefficiency, to get its strength organized. The lesson taught by Bull Run—that it was folly to try to make a campaign with an unprepared army—was still fresh in every man's mind. Autumn of 1861 was a time to get ready. Decisive action would have to come later.

But it is just possible, in spite of Belmont, that the Bull Run lesson had been learned a little too well. In Missouri, both Sterling Price and Nathaniel Lyon had demonstrated that great things could be done with the most grotesquely unready armies if the man in charge insisted on it. The Bull Run lesson needed to be interpreted in the light of two additional facts, which were not readily recognizable to the average professional. First, every Federal army, no matter how much it lacked in the way of training and equipment, was at least as well off in those respects as the army it was going to have to fight. Second, the Federal side did have an immense advantage in numbers, in war material, and in the capacity to make its losses good. That advantage was just as genuine an asset in the fall of 1861 as it was in the spring of 1864. It needed to be used.

It was used, presently, beginning in January, 1862, and what happened thereafter is instructive.

Albert Sidney Johnston, who commanded for the Confederates in the western theater, did not have nearly enough men to defend the long line that ran from the Mississippi River to the Cumberland Plateau, and he had held his ground throughout the fall simply by a skillful bluff which made his strength look much greater than it was.[6] When Grant and his naval coadjutor, Flag Officer Andrew Foote, insisted that this line be attacked at the earliest pos-

sible date they were simply reacting to a subconscious
knowledge of that fact, and between the two of them they
apparently persuaded the authorities to open an offensive
a little ahead of time. So Foote's gunboats promptly
knocked off Fort Henry, on the Tennessee—and Johnston's
whole line immediately collapsed. (For the record, of
course, it should be noted that George H. Thomas had already broken the eastern anchor of the line by winning the
battle of Mill Springs, or Logan's Cross Roads, in Kentucky.) Grant drove on to capture Fort Donelson, and
Johnston could do nothing but order an immediate retreat
and try to regroup in northern Mississippi.

Note that the driving force in this whole campaign came
from Grant. His superior officer, General Halleck, was obviously drawn into the campaign before he was quite ready;
and General Buell, who commanded for the Federals east
of the Tennessee River, went into action with even greater
reluctance, protesting that the thing had not been properly
prepared for and complaining bitterly because Grant forced
the occupation of Nashville before Buell was ready for it.
It was Grant, also, who believed that this victory ought to
be followed up with speed. Halleck restrained him—we must
pause in order to get everything arranged properly, there
must be due thought for reinforcements and lines of supply, it would be most risky to go plunging on before everybody is ready—and, as a result, the advance up the de-
fenseless Tennessee was made with much caution. In the
end Johnston was given seven weeks, which he did not
really need to be given, in order to bring his scattered
forces together at Corinth. Johnston used the time to good
advantage, and at Shiloh he struck a blow which nearly re-
dressed the balance.[7]

Admittedly, Shiloh does not show Grant at his best. He
displayed here the defects of his qualities. Eager to press
the advantage and overwhelm a beaten enemy, he thought
so much about the delayed offensive that he apparently

overlooked the fact that his enemy might launch a counter-offensive. When at last he was allowed to advance he advanced incautiously, and Johnston's massive counterstroke hit him before he was quite ready. The near-debacle at Pittsburg Landing needs to be interpreted in the light of the fact that if Grant had had his way the Federal army would have been ready to move forward from that bleak highland three weeks before the battle actually took place, at which time Johnston would have been in no shape to make an effective defense.

One more point needs to be made about Shiloh, and it highlights one more of Grant's characteristic traits. In the first day's fight, Grant's army unquestionably was defeated: but Grant himself was not defeated at all. Unforgettable, to any student of the battle, is General Sherman's account of meeting Grant at midnight, in the rain, after the first day's fight had ended. Grant was standing under a tree, keeping as dry as he could, puffing a cigar; Sherman came up to him, believing that the only possible course was to order a retreat the next morning, and said something to the effect that the day had been very tough and had gone badly. Grant nodded, bit his cigar, drew on it briefly, and then said: "Yes. Beat 'em in the morning, though." Grant, in other words, hung on, waited for Buell and Wallace to reinforce him, refused to think of withdrawal, made his counterattack on the second day, and in the end won one of the most significant Union victories of the entire war. After Shiloh, the Confederates in the west were doomed to a losing defensive.

Shiloh's gains, once more, were partly nullified by Halleck's caution. Halleck came on the scene a few days after the battle. He brought heavy reinforcements, so that before long the Federal army in northern Mississippi totaled approximately 125,000 men: Beauregard, commanding for the Confederates after Albert Sidney Johnston's battle death, had a scant 50,000. Halleck's army could have gone any-

where it chose. The heart of the South was open, and
Beauregard could not conceivably have made a stand-up
fight in opposition. But Halleck was a cautious, careful
professional, a man who knew war by the book rather than
by reality. He knew that Shiloh had almost been a disaster
because the Federals had been incautious and had not had
their defenses ready. In his advance, Halleck would not
make that mistake.

He edged forward with painstaking care, taking upward
of a month to make a 30-mile advance, and when Beauregard at last evacuated Corinth and retreated—there was
nothing else Beauregard could possibly have done—Halleck
split his forces into segments, devoting himself to the occupation of "strategic points," to the protection and repair
of railroad lines, to the consolidation of his position. The
great opportunity was missed. The Confederates were even
able before the summer was out to put on a counteroffen-
sive, which saw a Confederate army go nearly to the Ohio
River; to this day no one knows quite what that stroke
might have accomplished if it had been commanded by
anyone other than Braxton Bragg. The driving offensive
spirit which Grant gave his army evaporated once Halleck
got on the scene, and in consequence the Federal move to
open the Mississippi could not be resumed until nearly the
end of 1862.

Grant's Mississippi campaign, from its unhappy beginning
at Holly Spring to the final surrender of Pemberton's army
at Vicksburg on July 4, 1863, was of course one of the decisive strokes of the war—and one of the most brilliant. It is
interesting here simply because it shows Grant in a somewhat unfamiliar guise. His movement downstream from
Milliken's Bend, his crossing of the river, his lightning campaign to Jackson and back via Champion Hill to Vicksburg,
his ability to herd Pemberton into the isolated fortress and
to keep the Confederate relieving column under Joe
Johnston at arm's length until Pemberton at last had to give

up—this was one of the most dazzling campaigns of the entire war. It is interesting to note that in its beginning, at least, Grant did not have an advantage in numbers. When he crossed the river, cut loose from his base and marched into the interior, there were actually more Confederates than Unionists in Mississippi. The hoary assertion that Grant won victories simply because the odds were always heavily in his favor collapses here. This was a campaign in the Stonewall Jackson manner—great daring, fast and deceptive movement, hard blows struck at fragments of the opposing forces, ending in a victory which went far to determine the outcome of the entire war.

Whatever else it may have been, this campaign was not the campaign of a dull, unimaginative man who was a simple slugger and nothing more. Military genius was at work here. The Grant of the Vicksburg campaign was one of the great captains.

To midsummer of 1863, in other words, Grant's record is in the main excellent. He has carried out his assignments, learning his grim trade as he goes along, guided always by the offensive spirit, discovering along the way (at a high cost, admittedly) that the offensive needs to be leavened with a certain amount of caution; he has swallowed two opposing armies whole, he has opened the Mississippi Valley to the Union, and he has abundantly justified his belief that a Union general needs to apply the pressure to the Union's foes without a letup. It has worked. The war, as far as the Union is concerned, is over the peak.

The Chattanooga campaign, interesting as it is, must be recognized as more or less incidental. At Chattanooga, Grant was called on to do little more than pick up the pieces which had been dropped at the disastrous battle of Chickamauga. Grant took charge at Chattanooga at a time when the Union army had escaped the immediate threat of capture, which loomed so large immediately after the retreat from Chickamauga. All that was needed was a cool,

unhurried, business-like grasp of the situation and a determination to break out of the besieging ring as soon as everything was ready. This much Grant provided; it is extremely probable that George H. Thomas, left to himself,
would have provided it equally well, and although at the
time Grant's victory at Chattanooga struck Northerners as
a superlative achievement, the victory must be written
down simply as one which any competent Northern commander would have won under similar circumstances.
Probably Grant's matter-of-fact, common-sense coolness was
his chief asset here.

After Chattanooga, Grant's elevation to supreme command was inevitable. The step came early in the spring of
1864, when Grant was commissioned lieutenant-general
and was entrusted with the conduct of the nation's whole
military effort. All that had gone before was preparation;
now came the great challenge, the unlimited responsibility, the final time of testing. Any appraisal of Grant's qualities as a soldier must finally rest on what he did after the
supreme command was given to him.

What Grant did, beginning in the spring of 1864, was by
no means confined to Virginia. He stayed in Virginia, to be
sure, and the army that fought against Robert E. Lee was
known—against logic, and against military reality—as
"Grant's Army"; but the whole war was Grant's, and what
happened in Tennessee and in Georgia, and elsewhere, was
Grant's responsibility. And critiques of Grant's military capacity can grow a little foggy here, because the critic runs
the danger of succumbing to one of two oversimplifications.

The first one can be stated thus: Grant was responsible
for the grand strategy of the final year, the war was at last
won, and Grant therefore is a great soldier.

The other goes off in the opposite direction: Grant
fought against Lee with an overwhelming advantage in
numbers, took frightful losses, was never able to beat Lee
in the open field, won at last because he did have that ad-

vantage in numbers, and hence was simply a slugger who
came at last to victory because under the circumstances he
could hardly have come to anything else.

There is an element of truth in each oversimplification.
Neither one offers a proper evaluation of Grant's capacity.
Each one needs to be examined closely, and the two finally
need to be blended together.

It is entirely true that the grand strategy of the final
year, which worked, was Grant's. The war was not simply
Virginia; the western theater was part of it, too. Sherman's
armies moved remorselessly into the deep South, disem-
boweling the Confederacy, making it incapable of firm resistance, reducing that tragically beset nation to nothing
more than the territory between Richmond, Virginia, and
Raleigh, North Carolina, while still other armies mopped
up the outlying territories. This concept was Grant's, and
the responsibility was his. (If Sherman's bold march from
Atlanta to the sea had gone sour and had resulted in a lost
army and a fatal setback to the Union cause, the man who
would have had to shoulder the blame was Grant.) When
1864 began, the Confederacy lived because of two armies
—the Army of Northern Virginia under Lee, and the Army
of Tennessee, under Johnston. (There were other, lesser
armies elsewhere, but they were peripheral.) As long as
these two armies lived, the Confederacy would live; when
they were destroyed the Confederacy would die. It was
Grant who made those two armies the principal objectives
for the Federal war effort; it was Grant who saw to it that
the force needed to destroy those armies was mustered, supported, and relentlessly applied. If the grand strategy of the
war's final year worked, Grant is the man who is entitled to
take the bow. He had the authority to do these things, and
he used it up to the hilt. The result was victory.

At the same time, Grant's conduct of the campaign in
Virginia is extremely relevant to any appraisal of his abili-
ties, and it is clear that this campaign did not go quite as

Grant had hoped that it would go. His real aim when he planned the campaign was neither to capture Richmond nor to force the Confederate army into retreat; it was simply to destroy that army, and he hoped that he would be able to do it fairly quickly. Grant suspected, when he came east, that the Federal Army of the Potomac had somehow never been made to fight all-out. It had capacities, he believed, that had not quite been called on; he would call on them to the limit, and by unremitting aggressiveness would compel Lee to make a stand-up fight in which the superior Federal advantages in manpower and materiel would quickly win a decisive victory.

This, of course, did not happen. The campaign lasted very nearly a year, it was enormously costly to the Union army, and in the end it succeeded largely because the North could endure a long process of attrition better than the South could. Grant did not do what he set out to do; what he had been able to do against other Confederate commanders in the west he was not able to do against Lee. The long series of wearing, hideously expensive battles which in a few months almost destroyed the old fighting capacity of the Army of the Potomac lend some weight to the charge that Grant was an unimaginative bruiser who won, in the end, simply because he had overpowering numbers and used them remorselessly and without finesse.

So the Virginia campaign, which began when the Army of the Potomac crossed the Rapidan early in May, 1864, needs close examination.

One or two points need to be made clear at the beginning.

In the first place it is quite inaccurate to argue that no other Federal general ever enjoyed the over-all authority that was given to Grant when he became general-in-chief. McClellan had that authority, beginning in the fall of 1861 and running through the winter of 1862. Like Grant, he blocked out a comprehensive campaign covering all the important theaters of the war; the difference was that he could not make anything happen the way he wanted it to happen. He could not compel Halleck and Buell to work together, in the west. He could not make Buell drive into East Tennessee, although he repeatedly warned the man that his own strategy in Virginia depended on an aggressive advance by Buell's army. He could not even make his own army move according to his own timetable. If he was presently removed from over-all command of the Federal armies, the reason obviously was that he had not been able to exercise that over-all command effectively.

Halleck became general-in-chief early in the summer of 1862, and there is no question that President Lincoln hoped that he would be a vigorous commander. Halleck simply did not try to become one. The full authority Grant was finally given was Halleck's, when Halleck first came to Washington; but Halleck refused to reach out, seize it, and exercise it, and in a remarkably short time he had reduced himself to a sort of high-level advisor, a paper-shuffler who neither laid down nor enforced a comprehensive strategy for the war as a whole. President Lincoln rendered his own verdict on the man not long after the battle of Fredericksburg, when General Burnside wanted to renew the offensive and his principal subordinates disagreed violently. The army was immobilized as a result, and Lincoln wrote Halleck suggesting that he, as general-in-chief, go down to Fredericksburg, examine the situation, and then either tell Burnside to go ahead, with full support from the top, or call the whole business off and devise something else. "In this difficulty, if you do not help me," Lincoln wrote to Halleck, "you fail me precisely in the point for which I sought your assistance."[8]

This hurt Halleck's feelings, so that he offered to resign, and in the War Department files Lincoln's original letter presently got an addition, in the President's handwriting: "Withdrawn, because considered harsh by General Halleck." As commanding general, Halleck simply refused to function, and the overriding authority that had been given to him withered on the vine because he was incapable of using it. The point to remember, however, is that the authority was there for him to use if he had had the force to exert it.

In addition, the authority which was at last given to Grant was not really as all-inclusive as it is usually supposed to have been, a fact which had a profound effect on the course of military operations.

Grant did not have the full control which he is assumed to have had. He was not, for instance, able to cancel General Nathaniel Banks's ill-advised and desperately unlucky offensive along the Red River—an eccentric thrust which was political rather than military in its conception, which would not have accomplished a great deal even if it had succeeded, and which used men, ships, and materiel that might have been applied elsewhere to much better advantage. Grant had no use for this movement, but not until Banks ran into outright disaster was he able to get it withdrawn.

More important, Grant was not able to select the commanders for two very important subsidiary movements in Virginia: movements which were well conceived and which, if they had been handled skillfully, would almost certainly have enabled Grant to win over Lee the kind of victory he had counted on winning.

One Union army was ordered to proceed up the Shenandoah Valley, depriving the Army of Northern Virginia of the bountiful supplies which it got from that area and, eventually, threatening Richmond from the west. Another army was ordered to advance toward Richmond along the south bank of the James River. The movements of these two armies were as much a part of Grant's Virginia campaign as the movements of the Army of the Potomac itself. If they had gone as scheduled—as they might very well have done if they had been efficiently led—the job which had to be done by the Army of the Potomac would have been ever so much easier. Taken all together, the triple-headed campaign would have been something the Confederacy probably could not have met.

But Grant was not able to get men of his own choice to command either of these subsidiary offensives.

The army which moved up the Shenandoah was put under General Franz Sigel, who was about as completely incompetent a commander as the Union army possessed. Sigel got his job solely because his name had, or was thought to have, political value with the large German-born population. The year 1864 was an election year, and Washington decided that it was necessary to give Sigel prominence. And Sigel's Shenandoah campaign collapsed almost before it had got started. Sigel was dismally routed at New Market, and his army instead of helping the operations of the Army of the Potomac became a source of weakness.

It was the same with the advance up the James. This advance was entrusted to General Ben Butler, of whom it must be said that he was probably Sigel's equal in military incompetence; and Butler most certainly would not have been in command if Grant had had anything to say about it. Butler had the strength to drive right to the outskirts of Richmond, and if he had done this Lee would have been compelled to retreat, or to make ruinously expensive detachments of force, just when the Army of the Potomac was pressing him most severely. As it worked out, however, Butler completely missed his opportunity, and before long permitted himself to be penned up in defensive works at Bermuda Hundred. Lee did not have to detach troops to oppose Butler; on the contrary, Lee was presently reinforced by some of the troops whom Butler should have been keeping busy.

In other words, Grant's Virginia campaign did not go as he had planned it partly because the two subsidiary moves which were essential to the whole design were commanded by inept soldiers who would never have been allowed within miles of the field of operations if Grant had had his way. No appraisal of what Grant did in Virginia is complete if the abysmal failure of these two offensives is not taken into account.

Grant's authority, in other words, was not really as unadulterated as is generally supposed. If the armies in the Shenandoah and along the James had been commanded by real soldiers—by such men, for instance, as John Sedgwick (whom Meade originally proposed for the Shenandoah command) and W. F. Smith—it is obvious that the job which had to be done by Meade's army would have been much easier and, presumably, would have gone much more smoothly. Grant was handicapped by Washington's interference here precisely as McClellan was handicapped when he launched his own offensive in the spring of 1862.

In any case, Grant as general-in-chief made his headquarters with the Army of the Potomac and took that Army across the Rapidan and into the Wilderness on May 4, 1864.

We badly need a detailed examination of the command arrangements which resulted. The army of course was under General George Meade's immediate command. (In the beginning, Burnside's corps, which accompanied the army, was not under Meade's control, but this was rectified before much time had passed.) Grant was present at all times, his own headquarters staff and apparatus being camped, usually, within a short distance of Meade's. The situation undoubtedly was difficult for both commanders: in effect, the army had two heads, Meade was under constant supervision, and on a good many occasions Grant and his staff issued battle orders direct to Meade's subordinates. Both Meade and Grant did their best to make this cumbrous system work, but it unquestionably led to many difficulties.

These difficulties, in addition, were complicated by the fact that the Army of the Potomac was clique-ridden. Its officer corps contained many men who still felt that only McClellan was a really good commander. They tended to resent the arrival of Grant, the westerner, to question his ability on the ground that the successes he had won in the west had been won against second-raters, and to express open skepticism about his ability to accomplish anything against a soldier of Lee's caliber. (One of the interesting things about the men who enjoyed important commands in the Army of the Potomac was that they seem to have had more respect for Lee than for any of their own superiors.) It seems possible at times to detect a certain sluggishness in army movements arising from this fact. At the very least it must be said that the dual command arrangement was a handicap.[9]

Whether for this reason or for some other, control of the army at corps and divisional level seems to have been defective. The kind of quick, decisive moment which characterized the movements of Grant's army in the Vicksburg campaign, for example, was not in evidence. Cold Harbor was very poorly managed, and the whole attempt to seize Petersburg following the crossing of the James was hopelessly bungled; it is hardly too much to say that during the two or three crucial days in which that key point should have been occupied by Union forces the army as an army was hardly commanded at all. (Indeed, Meade himself said virtually as much, almost in so many words. On June 18, when he had his last chance to drive into Petersburg before Lee's army arrived, he found it utterly impossible to get a co-ordinated advance, and at last he burst out with the revealing telegram to his subordinates: "I find it useless to appoint an hour to effect co-operation . . . what additional orders to attack you require I cannot imagine. . . . Finding it impossible to effect co-operation by appointing an hour for attack, I have sent an order to each corps commander to attack at all hazards, and without reference to each other."[10]) The attack failed, naturally enough, and the Confederates held Petersburg for nine more months. It might be noted, in this connection, that the soldiers in the Army of the Potomac fought well enough here; the war weariness which is supposed to have resulted from Cold Harbor, and from the wearing campaign which had preceded it, had not yet set in. It was the army commander's failure to control the battle that was the trouble here.

The army commander, to repeat, was Meade: but Grant was the general-in-chief, he was with the army at the time, and as the man who would have gained the credit if a great victory had been won he can probably be given blame for the failure. It is hard to escape the conclusion that it was the dual command arrangement that was largely at fault . . . hard, also, to avoid the feeling that if a Sheridan or a Thomas had been in Meade's place during those first few days at Petersburg the story would have been different.

However all of that may have been, one more complaint about Grant's generalship in the Virginia campaign must be examined: the charge that he had too much faith in the virtues of a head-on offensive and failed to recognize the immense preponderance of the defensive in frontal assaults like the ones at Spotsylvania and Cold Harbor.

It is undoubtedly true that Grant underestimated the defensive strength of good troops, well entrenched, using rifled muskets. He shared this failing with most of the other Civil War generals, including Lee himself. Weapons used in the Civil War, even though they look extremely primitive today, were in fact much more modern than anything warfare had seen before. A revolution in tactics was taking place, and it took the generals a long time to realize it. One is tempted to speculate that the success of Thomas' great assault at Chattanooga, where a massed army corps captured the Missionary Ridge position which should have been completely invulnerable to any frontal attack, may have stuck too long in the back of Grant's mind. Whatever the reason, it must be said that it took Grant a long time to see that the all-along-the-line attack after the old manner was out of date. A great many men died because of this.[11]

Summing up the criticisms of the Virginia campaign of 1864, then, one must say: (1) that the subsidiary campaigns which should have insured the success of the advance of the Army of the Potomac failed miserably because Grant was unable to control the appointment of the men who led them; (2) that the command arrangement which grew out of his insistence on accompanying Meade's army was most defective and probably was at least partly responsible for a number of costly setbacks; and (3) that Grant himself showed too much fondness for old-fashioned offensive combat when the conditions under which that kind of combat could have succeeded had disappeared.

Against these criticisms, balance Grant's achievements. They are more solid than is apparent at first glance.

First of all, and perhaps most important of all, Grant was the one Federal general, from first to last, who kept the initiative in the Virginia theater.

Each one of his predecessors had moved South in a great "Forward to Richmond" campaign, and each one of them had found before long that he had lost the ball and was on the defensive; instead of forcing Lee to keep step with him, the Federal general was always trying to keep step with Lee, usually without great success. McClellan, Pope, Burnside, Hooker, even Meade—each one went south to defeat a strongly outnumbered opponent and before long found either that he was in full retreat or that he was fighting desperately for survival. Here was the fact that had given the generals in the Army of the Potomac such vast respect for Lee's military ability. No matter how a campaign began, it usually ended with Lee calling the shots.

The second achievement grows out of the first.

By keeping the initiative, Grant compelled Lee to fight

the kind of war which Lee could not win. Lee's conduct of
the campaign which began in the Wilderness and ended at
last in front of Petersburg was masterly, enormously costly
in Northern lives, almost ruinous to home-front morale—the
profound wave of war weariness which swept the North in
the summer of 1864 came largely because the Virginia campaign was so dreadfully expensive and seemed to be accomplishing so little—but it did end with Lee locked up in
a fortress where effective offensive movements were impossible for him. Not long after the Wilderness campaign began, Lee remarked that if he were ever forced back into
the Richmond lines and compelled to stand on the defensive
there the end would be only a matter of time.[12] He was,
in spite of his best efforts, forced back into those lines; in
spite of his magnificent tactical successes, the process took
only a little more than six weeks; and after that it was, as
Lee himself had predicted, just a question of time.

The campaign did, to be sure, reduce the fighting capacity of the valiant Army of the Potomac to a low level. Such
excellent combat units as Hancock's II Corps, for example,
late in the summer became almost impotent; at Reams Sta-
tion this corps was routed by a Confederate counterattack
which the same corps would have beaten off with ease six
months earlier. But this grim process of attrition worked
both ways. The Army of Northern Virginia was worn down
also, so that it likewise became unable to do things which
in earlier years it would have done smoothly. The Federal
cause could endure this attrition and the Southern cause
could not.

Yet it was not actually just a campaign of attrition. The
significant thing is that Lee was deprived of the opportunity
to maneuver, to seize the openings created by his opponent's
mistakes, to make full use of the dazzling ability to combine
swift movements and hard blows which had served him so
well in former campaigns. Against Grant, Lee was not able

to do the things he had done before. He had to fight the sort of fight he could not win.

Finally, even though Grant's original hope was to bring Lee to battle in the open and destroy his army, he was really conducting an immense holding operation, and what happened in Virginia means nothing unless it is examined in the light of what was happening elsewhere. Sherman was advancing in and through Georgia. Unless the Confederacy could intervene against him, Sherman would eventually provide the winning maneuver. Grant held Lee down so effectively that intervention against Sherman became impossible; holding Lee, Grant insured Sherman's victory. When Sherman won, the war was won. Lee, to be sure, held out to the bitter end, but the end came because the Confederacy behind Lee had shrunk to a helpless fragment.

It gets back, in other words, to the grand strategy, the concept of the war as a whole in which the movements of all of the Federal armies were interrelated. What Grant did in Virginia enabled the grand strategy to work. Viewed in that light, the Virginia campaign was a success: costly, agonizing, all but unendurably grueling in its demands on soldiers and on the people back home, but still a success.

Grant, in short, was able to use the immense advantage in numbers, in military resources, and in money which the Federal side possessed from the start. Those advantages had always been there, and what the Northern war effort had always needed was a soldier who, assuming the top command, would see to it that they were applied steadily, remorselessly and without a break, all across the board. The complaint that Grant succeeded only because he had superior numbers is pointless. The superior numbers were part of the equation all along. It was Grant who took advantage of them and used them to apply a pressure which the weaker side could not possibly stand.

This was a most substantial achievement. Achieving it,

Grant merits very high ranking as a soldier. He used the means at hand to discharge the obligation which had been put upon him. The war was won thereby, and it is not easy to see how it would have been won without Grant.

### NOTES

1. Lee to Governor John Letcher, December 26, 1861, *Southern Historical Society Papers,* I (1876), 462.

2. *War of the Rebellion: A Compilation of the Official Records of the Union and Confederate Armies* (Washington, 1880–1901), Series I, Vol. XVI, part 1, p. 51. Cited hereafter as *Official Records;* all references are to Series I.

3. Speech of John A. Rawlins, in the *Proceedings of the Society of the Army of the Tennessee* (Cincinnati, 1866).

4. *Personal Memoirs of U. S. Grant* (New York, 1885), I, 273–74; A. L. Conger, *The Rise of U. S. Grant* (New york, 1931), pp. 99–101.

5. John W. Emerson, "Grant's Life in the West," *Midland Monthly Magazine,* VI (1896).

6. Edward A. Pollard, *The Lost Cause* (New York, 1866), p. 202.

7. Details regarding the delays in the Union advance preceding Shiloh are summarized in this writer's *Grant Moves South* (Boston, 1960), pp. 210–15.

8. *Official Records,* XXI, 940, 944–45, 953–54.

9. Peter S. Michie, *The Life and Letters of Emory Upton* (New York, 1885), pp. 108–9; James H. Wilson, *Under the Old Flag* (New York, 1912), I, 400.

10. *Official Records,* XL, 167, 179, 205.

11. There is an excellent discussion of the effect on Civil War tactics of improved firepower in J. F. C. Fuller, *The Generalship of Ulysses S. Grant* (London, 1929).

12. Douglas Southall Freeman, *R. E. Lee* (New York, 1934–35), III, 398.

# A New Appraisal*

## 1958

When Lloyd Lewis sat down to write a biography of General William Tecumseh Sherman, it is probable that the last thing in his mind was the desire to set a new trend in American literature. He was writing about a man who interested him greatly, he thought that what ought to be said about that man had not yet been said, and he undertook—with deep understanding, and great literary skill—to say it in his own way. Nevertheless, his book did set things moving in a new direction. Indeed, in a quiet way it constitutes something of a landmark in the story of the Civil War.

Lewis wrote *Sherman, Fighting Prophet* in 1932. For fully a quarter-century before that, Northerners who wrote about the Civil War had been doing their utmost to be judicious, fair-minded, unemotional and nonpartisan. One can find nothing but praise for that attempt; the only trouble with the men who made it was that they were altogether too successful. They did what they set out to do, and as a result the blood went out of what they wrote. They were Americans, born no more than half a century after America's greatest single trial by blood and fire; and what they wrote concern-

* *Sherman, Fighting Prophet* by Lloyd Lewis, Harcourt, Brace & Company, 1932, 1958

ing that time of trial might as well have been written about the Trojan War, as far as any sign of emotional involvement on the part of the writers was concerned. Detachment in a writer can be an excellent quality, but when it proceeds to the point where the writer has lost touch with the blood and flesh of his subject it is time for someone to call a halt. Writing about Sherman, Lloyd Lewis called the halt, and Northern literature concerning the Civil War has been different ever since.

Lewis shared one quality with the Southerners who had been writing about the war: he cared about it with a deep and moving intensity. It meant something to him. The men who fought in it were not bloodless people out of some old book, but living men who had been bred on his own soil, who shared his own hopes and passions and frailties, and who when they went to war were moved by aspirations and emotions in which he himself had a portion. Some of their aspirations and emotions may have been sadly muddled, some of the things they did may have been deplorable by any abstract standard, the net worth of what they accomplished may still be open to dispute—no matter, they were people whom he understood and for whom he felt a profound kinship, and he put all of it down as a man who, no matter what else he may have known, at least understood to the ultimate limit the inner feelings of the soldiers of long ago who had endured much and who had accomplished much.

Writers from the South had never needed to rediscover that quality, because they had never lost it. They cared, they felt, and they translated that caring and feeling in what they wrote. From John Esten Cooke down to Douglas Southall Freeman, no one was ever in the slightest doubt where their inner loyalties lay. They could make the reader see how the Confederate leader or the Confederate follower felt because they had that feeling themselves; intellectually, they might admit that the Lost Cause was well and properly lost, but it at least remained in their eyes a Cause which still had the glow and the warmth that led men to die for it.

Feeling so, they brought to their writing something of the warmth and immediacy which come from actual experience of the thing described. That most of them were born long after the war ended made no difference; they had absorbed it, partly by long emotional identification with the men and the cause they were writing about, and partly by wide acquaintance with the old men who, years before, had fought in the war. This quality Lloyd Lewis had, and it lifted *Sherman, Fighting Prophet* to a level which few twentieth-century Northern accounts had attained.

It may be that complete objectivity is not the most notable virtue which an account of the Civil War can possess. The war will always remain just a little mysterious. It came somehow out of what people a century ago were, it took its shape and its color from them, it was like no other experience America ever had, and it remains something to read about and to dream about because, in a queer but compelling way, it reveals something fundamental about the American spirit. The sober analyses of social trends, economic forces, political tensions, and strategic planning may continue until doomsday; we will not get a complete picture unless we begin by establishing an emotional kinship with the men who fought the war.

In one of his acknowledgments printed in *Myths After Lincoln*, Lewis wrote this sentence: "To certain pioneers such as Joseph Rogers, Ziba Darlington, Noah Haines and T. M. Hardy, veterans of the Army of the Tennessee, who have long been dead under little Union flags in the Friends' graveyard at Spring Valley, Indiana, but who, in their lifetimes, would tell an inquisitive boy what they remembered . . ." The inquisitive boy listened, remembered, and was deeply stirred; and when he himself came to write—about the doings of young men quaintly named Ziba and Noah, who came from a very youthful America and who took part in the enormous struggle which helped that youthful America become mature—he was able to convey to a modern generation a sense of what those men were like and what was chiefly moving them. As Marc Connelly put it, in his remarks at a memorial service for Lewis in 1949:

"That was why Lloyd could walk in comradeship with the men of the Civil War. That was why when we join Lloyd in discovering Sherman . . . we are identified with the time, with the places, the smells, and the sights and sounds of those who are only, in a physical sense, of the past."

Which brings us to General Sherman, about whom Lewis wrote so eloquently.

Connelly was right; essentially, this book is a discovery of Sherman. The famous soldier had been written about before, and he has been written about since, and on the surface there seems to be very little mystery about him, because he was uncommonly articulate. He never hesitated to say exactly what he thought; he had thoughts on practically every subject under the sun, and they are all in the record somewhere. Yet Sherman somehow proved a hard man to understand. He was the destroyer, the wrecker, the hard man of great wrath who saw himself as the agent appointed to chastise men for their follies. At the same time he had a deep inner feeling for the very people whom he was smiting so relentlessly; he had almost no share in the spirit of hatred and revenge which rose to the top in the North as the war drew to a close, and in the end he nearly ruined his own career by his effort to bring about a peace of reconciliation and understanding, in which that which had been destroyed could be rebuilt. He could be, and often was, as bitterly critical of Northern leaders as of Southern; he professed very little use for many of the folkways of democracy, not until near the end of the war did he reach an understanding of what Abraham Lincoln was really up to, and there have been few great Americans who placed less value on the freedom of the press. (When he was told that it was necessary to

have correspondents with the army, because the families of
the soldiers needed to be told what was going on, he
snorted indignantly: all of the soldiers, he said, wrote regularly to their families, and their letters would give the
people back home all of the news they really needed to get.)
He could be pitiless, as a warrior, and when he prepared to
make his first attack at Vicksburg and was warned that the
attack would cost many Union casualties he remarked coldly
that it was going to cost 5000 men to get into Vicksburg and
that the price might as well be paid now as later. Yet it was
the same Sherman who, barely a year earlier, lost his command and was publicly branded as a lunatic because he
could not live with the thought of taking unprepared boys
into battle against what he considered to be excessive odds.

Sherman was, in other words, a man of contradictory aspects, and the great virtue of Lewis's book is that it shows
how those different aspects became a part of the man's character and how they finally were welded into a coherent
whole. Lewis was able to do this partly because he had
studied everything Sherman did and said with perceptive
care, and partly because he always saw Sherman as expressing the inner spirit of the unsophisticated, poorly trained,
matter-of-fact young men who fought under him. Not the
least of the values in *Sherman, Fighting Prophet* is the fact
that it tells as much about Sherman's soldiers as it tells about
Sherman himself. Lewis went straight to the sources. He had
talked with the old veterans himself; also, he had read their
letters and diaries, and he was one of the first to exploit that
invaluable mine of material that lies buried in the informal
regimental histories which were written in such numbers, a
generation after the war, by innumerable survivors' associations. His account of the Battle of Shiloh, for instance, is a
classic, but the focus here is only partly on Sherman himself,
even though it was in this terrible fight that Sherman found
himself as a soldier. What one remembers best about Lewis's
account of this battle is his picture of the enlisted man, who

was pitched unready into a ferocious two-day fight and who, like the general himself, learned his trade there and was forever after a different sort of person.

In a sense, Sherman's story—like the story of any Civil War general—was the story of the men whom he led; and throughout this book the men who were led (and who, every so often, showed an astounding capacity for leading themselves when the notion struck them) play a leading part. And they play that part because Lewis *knew* them and knew that the general cannot be understood unless the enlisted man is understood as well. The story of the famous march to the sea, for instance—which, all things considered, is not one of the prettiest stories in the American album—is utterly incomprehensible unless one has a clear picture of the soldiers who made the march. The wholesale destruction that was inflicted on a portion of Georgia, and later on luckless South Carolina, was derived only in part from the commanding general; much of it came straight out of the rowdy, devil-may-care, irrepressible young men in blue who suddenly discovered that what had been serious war had changed into a monstrous Halloween frolic in which practically all rules were off. No one who recalls what used to happen on Halloween in Midwestern small towns in an earlier generation will ever be perplexed in the effort to understand what happened in Georgia when Sherman marched down to the sea.

It remains to be said that as a study of Sherman, this book stands up remarkably well. Few military students have ever found a better sentence to sum up the occasionally baffling characteristic of Sherman as a soldier than Lewis's simple comment that the man never fully won a battle or lost a campaign. Sherman was a most able soldier, but he was not cast in the traditional mold. He understood modern war better than most of his contemporaries—indeed, he should have understood it, because he helped to invent it. He would have been at home with modern weapons and modern strategic concepts; given a few days to understand what airplanes, motor trucks, tanks, and so on can really do, he would have known how to use them, with no regrets for the lost glories of war in the old manner.

How far was Sherman consciously trying to put through Lincoln's own ideas about peace when he gave General Joe Johnston the surrender terms which the Federal government later felt obliged to disavow? Lewis felt that Sherman had a precise picture of what Lincoln wanted and that when he himself came under criticism and saw his work canceled he refused to offer an alibi, preferring to take the responsibility for his acts himself rather than to try to "throw off" on the dead president. The case may have been slightly overstated; Sherman unquestionably believed that he was doing what Lincoln would have wished, but that he had definite instructions in that respect is probably to be doubted. It matters very little. The man who had made hard war tried his best to make a soft peace and was rebuked for it. Considering the difficulties which grew out of the peace that was finally made, one is compelled to wonder if Sherman's plan was quite as defective as contemporary opinion thought it was.

Near the end of his life, Lloyd Lewis was working on a projected biography of General U. S. Grant, and he said once that as a result of his study of Grant he might eventually have to recast certain portions of *Sherman, Fighting Prophet*. He did not, apparently, feel that he had discovered anything that would cause any basic change in the book. What was bothering him seems to have been the feeling that much of the Sherman story can be fully understood only by an examination of the Grant-Sherman relationship. Grant brought Sherman out, as a man and as a soldier, and Lewis once remarked that he felt like calling his first Grant volume "The Education of W. T. Sherman." More, perhaps, than any two soldiers in American history, Grant and Sherman went together. They understood each other, and (which was even more important) they understood the section that had produced them, the new, sprawling, untidy, and incomprehensibly energetic Middle West. Lewis shared in that understanding, which is one of the reasons why this book will endure.

For Lewis's study of Sherman is, by any standard, one of the lasting contributions to Civil War literature. It brings understanding of the man himself and of his time; best of all, it helped to restore to Northern writing on the greatest of America's wars the sense of emotional involvement, the realization that deep feelings and far-reaching ideals were involved, the feeling that in examining the war we are touching human beings with whom, if we permit ourselves, we can still walk in understanding and kinship.

# The End of the Centennial*

## 1967

This observance is unique. I think this is the first time in history that the surviving veterans of a great war got together a full century later and spent four years celebrating their own achievements.

For complete historical accuracy, of course, it must be admitted that none of us actually fought in that war. We just feel as if we had. Sometimes we have fought about it. In any case, we have lived through it. Most of us, I suppose, began to do that long before the centennial came. And it must be added that we were all volunteers. We signed up for the duration. When the great test of the centennial came, we rallied to the flag; indeed, we rallied to both flags at once. Our patriotic fervor was leavened with a fine sense of impartiality. And we stuck to the finish. We took certain casualties along the way, some of us acquired war scars, there is a great deal of combat fatigue—but at least we saw it through. About all that remains is to find out about the pensions. We have been at it, in other words, for a long time.

A historian once advised his students that when they ex-

* A Portion of That Field, The Centennial of the Burial of Lincoln, University of Illinois Press, 1967

amined the people of any particular period in the past they should "study them until you can hear them talking." Most of us participating in this event, I suppose, have done that. We got personally acquainted with those soldiers of so long ago; got so well acquainted that we have heard them talking. They came alive for us, and we listened to them and I think we learned something thereby. In a way the whole centennial commemorative effort has been an exercise, by the entire country, in trying to hear what the men of the 1860s have to say to us.

They have had a good deal to say, and as we come now to the end of the centennial observance I think it is worth our while to sum up what we have all learned. It is time for such a summing-up. This is muster-out time—or, if you prefer, the time of parole. To paraphrase General Grant's famous sentence, we can now return to our homes, not to be disturbed by the centennial authorities so long as we observe our paroles and the laws that are in force where we reside. Before we go, however, let's look back and see what we got out of it all. What was this four-year centennial worth to the nation that sponsored it? Did we, as a country, get anything out of it worth all of the time, money, and effort that were put into it?

Perhaps the most striking single fact about this whole business, to begin with, is that our observance of the one hundredth anniversary of the Civil War is an event unique in history. When, at any time or place recorded in the annals of history, have all of the people of a proud nation gathered together, by mutual consent, to commemorate the memory of a *civil war*? That is the sort of thing that never happens. Civil wars are things people want to forget. I have never heard of Englishmen and Scotsmen getting together to make fraternal speeches on the field of Culloden, or of any great pageant staged at Naseby; or all of France pausing in its other concerns to relive the events connected with the Paris Commune in 1870; or of Irishmen and Englishmen making a pleasant holiday out of ceremonies connected with the Battle of Boyne. It just does not happen.

Civil wars are the worst of all wars. They raise memories that are best laid quietly to rest. Their effects remain as scar tissue; often enough, as a matter of fact, the wounds they create really never do heal, the hatreds and antagonisms that caused and were increased by rebellion never die out but remain generation after generation to breed a sullen anger and suspicion that at last become wholly poisonous. Never do the descendants of the contending parties find that their common memories of their time of contention are something that both sides like to relive—even to the extent of donning the old uniforms again, unfolding the old flags, and re-enacting the very battles that once drove them apart. Never—except that it did work out that way with us.

The memory of our Civil War has not been a divisive force in this country. On the contrary, it has been a source of unity—something that ties us together and gives us a new depth of mutual understanding. Incredibly, the greatest and most terrible war we ever fought—the one we fought with each other—has given us greater strength and a more enduring unity. It has given us a common tradition, shared memories that go to the very roots of our existence as a people. The most remarkable single fact about the centennial observance that is now ending is that it was held at all. It was not imposed by decree or undertaken from any sense of duty. It was simply something we all wanted to do.

Shared memories of this kind are extremely important, especially in a land whose origins are as diverse as ours. Our national history is not, after all, very long, and every nation and race on earth is represented among us; yet we have not become what might have been expected from such a situation—a mere conglomeration of separate peoples, bound together by nothing much stronger than geography and the accidents of economic interest. We are perhaps the most cohesive people on earth, bound together by ties that cannot be broken or even weakened, and I believe the greatest single reason for this is our intense absorption in our own history. We have a deep and enduring consciousness of our own past; more than anything else, that is what makes us Americans. If our national tradition is comparatively brief it is extremely powerful. And the largest, most compelling, and ultimately the most consequential chapter in that historical tradition of ours is the story of our Civil War.

We look back on it for many reasons; the foremost, perhaps, is our own universal recognition that when the worst that can be said about the Civil War has been said, that war remains as the stupendous price America paid to break its way into the modern world. During the past century our country not only entered the modern world but came to lead it, almost to dominate it. It had always had a great potential; what the Civil War did was make it certain that the potential would be freed to develop to its utmost. Because of that experience of ours—so painful, acquired at such terrible expense—we found ourselves committed to a course of development unlike any other in history: we got the opportunity, along with the obligation, to develop to the utmost the infinite material capacities of modern man, hand in hand with the infinite possibilities that develop out of human freedom. Taken together, these make a powerful combination. So far we have hardly done more than scratch the surface in either of these directions, but the opportunity is still there —along with the obligation. I think great days are ahead of us.

These, to be sure, might have come anyway, without the war—later, perhaps, and in a different way. They *did* come to us, however, from the Civil War, and that is one great reason it has been so worth our while to look back on the experience.

Now there is another angle to consider here. We agree that our experience has been blessedly unique in that we have been able to make a great asset out of something that might well have been a profound and crippling liability. How did it happen that way? What were some of the direct, tangible reasons for our quick development of this attitude? *Why* has our memory of the Civil War served to tie us together rather than to drive us apart?

Precisely here we owe something to General Ulysses S. Grant and to General Robert E. Lee. When those two men met at Appomattox a century ago they served their reunited country very well indeed. For they made, supported, and led all others to support a little document that could be the basis of a genuine peace of reconciliation. By what they did there they set the terms for the peace: No reprisals on the one hand, full acceptance of the result on the other. The thing to bear in mind here is that civil wars usually don't end that way. They bring an imposed peace that has to be supported by force for years, sometimes forever, and the settlement usually intensifies the passions that brought the trouble in the first place. It was not so at Appomattox. Grant rode back to his army and, as his first act, angrily stopped his men from firing salutes to their own success, on the commonsense ground (so very, very rare at the end of a great rebellion) that the men who had just surrendered were fellow countrymen again and ought to be accepted as such.

And Lee returned to his own army, composed a brief, temperate address telling his men to accept what had happened and to look to their future as citizens of a nation they had tried so hard to tear apart. Then he rode quietly off into legend. It is that legend that I would like to discuss briefly now.

The Confederate legend has grown mightily in the last century, until now it is a possession of the entire country, although of course it is revered most mightily in the South. It began to grow the moment Lee turned Traveller's head away from Appomattox, and it has been growing ever since, until now it is a mighty, omnipresent force in the

land. You are all familiar with it. It begins with Lee, the
deified man done in bronze on a bronze horse, incapable
of error or human frailty, abiding forever in the Valhalla
(whose membership is extraordinarily small, when you stop
to think about it) of Americans who may not be criticized
or questioned. And the Confederate soldier followed him
into the same legend as the incredibly gallant, heroic long-
suffering mortal who triumphed over fatigue, over hardship,
over the terrors of battle, over everything except the force
of superior numbers and who went down to defeat at last
conscious that he had done all a brave man could do for a
cause that was wholly unspotted. That, in its barest outline,
is the legend of the Lost Cause.

Now I would like to suggest to you, in all seriousness,
that this legend of the Lost Cause has been an asset to the
entire country. Contrast what was with what might have
been, remembering as you do that the heritage of a civil war
is almost universally a heritage of bitterness and fury. The
people of the South had battled to the limit of endurance
for four years against a power that was at last too strong
for them. They had built up a reserve of emotional involvement that could have found a most desperate outlet. The
Civil War could so easily have brought about a state of incurable guerilla warfare, with eternal enmity proclaimed by
crossroads ambushes and midnight reprisals, with dragoons
harrying the countryside across state after state, tamping
down each outburst but at the same time increasing the pressure that would evoke another explosion. Hand in hand with
this would have gone unending plots and conspiracies; the
war itself would have been ended, but it would not have
been *settled*. An incurable sore would have been created
that men would hardly even try to heal, and in the end in-
calculable damage would have been inflicted on the entire
nation. The Civil War might very conceivably have been a
tragedy from which our country could never have recovered.

That this did not happen was of course due to a large extent to Lee himself. He saw that danger, spoke against it, flatly refused to countenance any suggestion that the struggle be kept alive after the formal fighting had ended, and threw his immense influence into the scales on the side of peace and reconciliation.

But I think another important factor was the Confederate legend itself. I suspect that it became a most important channel through which the deep emotional currents that flowed across the southland were led off into a region where they could never again provoke violence. The glorification of the Lost Cause drew a great part of its strength from the fact that the loss itself was admitted and accepted. It contained no hint that enmity should be kept alive and that the wrongs of war should be avenged. It became a form of adjustment to a reality that was unpleasant; the passion that might so easily have poisoned American life forever spiraled off, or at least the major part of it did, into the enshrinement of a beautiful and romantic legend which over the years has been a most useful thing for the country as a whole. It has saved us, indirectly but effectively, a great deal of trouble.

By saying all of this I, of course, do not mean to imply that a reign of universal love and brotherhood dawned the moment the armies finished their business at Appomattox. That resentments still exist I do not doubt. That a certain emotional gap still remains between Yankees and Southerners is beyond question a fact of present-day life. What I am saying is that we did not get out of that war something that it would have been impossible to live with. We got something people could manage, something they could handle, and the very intensity of the Confederate legend has been one of the most helpful factors.

One more point remains. I believe that these centennial years have given us a new understanding of our own past and of each other, and these things are of very great importance. But during these years we have come to see one other thing more clearly than we saw it before. The war not only gave us a new base for unity and a deeper realization of the part that unity must play in our national life; it also greatly broadened the base of human freedom, and it left us with the great obligation to see that a proper edifice is built on that base. The war did end human slavery; ending it, it made all men free and left us compelled to understand that freedom in America is as indivisible as it is universal, that it is secure for the most fortunate only if at the same time it is secure for the least fortunate. Our Declaration of Independence begins with the flat assertion that all men are created equal; the Civil War closed with the flat assertion that equality has to be made good.

We study the people until we can hear them talking. One participant in the Civil War we ought to start listening to is the Negro. He was central, in that war. If his existence as a slave was not precisely the cause of the war, it was at least a factor without which the war would not have taken place. The Negro was what the war was about, somehow, and any attempt to define what the war means must take him into account. I suggest that we listen to him for a moment.

In 1863 the Federal government maintained an immense concentration camp—really, there is no other word for it— somewhere in Arkansas. It was a horrible place. Anything you can find in the record about the terrors of prison camps like Andersonville or Elmira pales into nothing when compared with the record of this place. It was a fearful place of trial for people who blindly, dumbly, but led on by an indomitable hope, were trying to climb from their place below the bottom rung of the ladder. They came to this camp and were treated so badly that some of them actually elected to go back into slavery in the belief that Simon Legree could do nothing to them which would be as bad as what their liberators were doing. Some good people in the North tried to help them by sending gifts of clothing. Now it happened that these refugees from slavery had children with them, and the death rate for these children, in the unsanitary camps where they were poorly fed and given little medical care, was appalling. The people who distributed clothing to these refugees soon noticed an odd fact. When a child died (which happened all the time) the parents would take the best garments that had been given to them in order to clothe the child for burial. Those supervisors who cared about such things tried to reason with them, explaining that this clothing, after all, was for the living; the dead children would not be helped by wearing it into their graves. The Negroes understood this well enough, but their answer was unvarying: "Yes, we know, but we want them to look pretty." Study them until you can hear them talking. That way comes understanding.

Now the plight of the colored man, in and after the war, goes to the very heart of our existence as a nation. He was given the right to full freedom and equality because of the war, but this right has never been made good. This failure means that reforms must be made, not merely in some of our laws and customs, but in our own hearts as well. Because of the Civil War, we are obliged to grapple with, and to destroy, the evil of race prejudice. By removing slavery the Civil War left that evil out on the counter, naked and un-disguised, and now it is ours to deal with. This is not a south-ern problem; all of you know very well that it is poisonous in the North as well. The job of conquering it, so that free-dom and equality may be the rule everywhere in the land, is with us in Springfield as in Selma. It is the unfinished business left with us by that war whose centennial we are now closing. I suggest that it is time we got on with it.

So what is left to us, as the centennial period closes? We have what we began with: memories of a great and tragic experience. One memory that molded us as a people and left us with a great responsibility; one also that is lit with purple shadows and touched by the voices of people who lived long before we were born and who speak somehow of the America they served and loved, the America it is ours to honor. They left us, too, with a sense of mission, a realization that we have an obligation to the past and to the future which we must in the end live up to.

On the last day of his life, Good Friday, April 14, 1865, Abraham Lincoln told members of his cabinet about a strange dream he had had the night before. He dreamed, he said, that he was on a mysterious ship, moving rapidly over an uncertain sea toward what he described as "a dark and indefinite shore." He considered this an omen of some sort, and indeed it was: He went to Ford's Theatre that night, and Booth shot him to death. The strange gift of second sight apparently came to this man, once in a while, but this one time it gave him something he could not quite interpret.

We are left just slightly in his predicament. His dream is still an omen: A full century later, we are on that mysterious vessel, moving across an uncertain sea toward a dark and indefinite shore—a shore for which there is no chart, because no man has ever seen it. Yet we do know a little something about it. It is the shore of that undiscovered country toward which America has been bound from the beginning: a country in which the noblest dreams Americans have ever had will come closer to being true simply because all of us share in them. We have had four years of looking back, now it is time to look ahead. Whether we reach the shore is up to us. We have only to live up to our past and to do our honest best to lay our hands on the magnificent future which that past lights up for us.

*II*

# History as Literature*

Any man who undertakes to talk about history as literature ought to begin by expressing his deep conviction that when it becomes literature history does not in any way cease to be history.

We have not, in other words, met to hear a defense of "popularized history," or to talk about the once-over-lightly operation that comes when a man who has read eight or ten books concludes that the Lord has appointed him to take this stuff and put a bead on it. We do no more than measure our own confusion if we assume that history as literature must be something less than history taken straight, at 100 proof.

The first trouble, however, is that it is so hard to say just what 100 proof history actually is. The simplest approach probably is to say that true history is simply the record of what really happened, and that would be a fine definition if we could just be sure that we can ever actually get such a record. Unfortunately, most of the time we cannot be sure. History is something less than a science, even though its practitioner does need the scientific approach. Its areas

* An address to the Society of American Historians, McGraw-Hill Book Company

of absolute certainty are small and there is very little chance
to make them larger.

For the historian always finds himself with a great deal of
data that do not quite fit into an equation whose literal, final
truth can be demonstrated once and for all beyond the pos-
sibility of error. He is of course looking for the unvarnished
truth, but he is always handicapped and sometimes entirely
frustrated by the fact that very little truth is really unvarnished and by the additional fact that it can be extremely
hard to tell truth from half-truth or even from outright falsehood. Even when he lays his hands on solid facts, they are
not of much use to him until he is prepared to say what they
meant to the people who lived with them; he not only needs
to know what men did but why they did it and what the
results of their doing it may have caused other people to do;
and while this pursuit is one of the most fascinating pursuits
open to man it does not often lead to clear, biblical certainty.

The historian, in short, is dealing with human beings, with
the leaders and the led, with what men thought and believed
and what their thoughts and beliefs finally resulted in, and
some of the things he most needs to know are forever locked
up in the minds and hearts of men who had been dead for a
long time. He is looking for realities, but usually the most
he can do is to trace the shadows those by-gone realities
once cast. Some of the evidence he needs is bound to be
missing, and the rest of it usually need a great deal of sifting,
and in the end the historian has to grapple as best he can
with a handful of intangibles. Whatever he writes is always
subject to revision by someone who comes along a little
later.

But this is only part of the problem. For if the historian
who wants to inscribe the record of "what really happened"
is writing about people, whose ways are always just a little
bit incomprehensible, he is also writing *for* people, even if
he narrows his field so sharply that the only people he cares

about are other historians. He is trying, in other words, not merely to get a story together but to tell it; to use the jargon of our own time and place, he is trying to communicate something. His very existence implies the existence of an audience which he hopes to reach. His audience may be small and it may be highly specialized, but he does want to interest it. Whether he realizes it or not—whether he likes it or not—at the moment he puts the paper in his typewriter he is committing himself to literature.

Now it may well be true that literature, considered by and large, enters the field of creative art little farther than history enters the field of true science, but the approach is what matters. The historian who collects, appraises, selects and analyzes his facts is bound to use the scientific approach even though the data he works with may not be the immutable building blocks of science; in the same way, when he undertakes to put his findings into words he is bound to attempt the artistic approach simply because he does want other men to read what he is writing, and to succeed he is obliged to use the skills of the creative artist. To be sure, he may not desire to stir the emotions of his readers —to lift them out of themselves, to arouse them to a new understanding of life, of the universe and of man's bewildering place in both—but at the very least he is trying to reach inside of their minds and show them the truth as he has found it. However matter-of-fact he may be about his job, he is actually trying to do what Kipling set forth as the eternal goal of the artist: "To draw the Thing as he sees it, for the God of Things as they are." Like Molière's gentleman who discovered to his delight that he had been talking prose all his life without knowing it, he finds if he looks into matters that he is unintentionally practicing literature.

Now of course the field of history is so broad that it contains a good deal of material that is not and never can be substantial literature. Our knowledge of the past is enriched by the patient, laborious efforts of men who bring vast knowledge and much time to bear on the scrutiny of small, comparatively unimportant fragments of the historic record. For instance: a man may spend years grubbing through courthouse files and the records of business firms that no longer exist in order to shed one ray of light on the relationship between the Alabama cotton trade in 1860 and Alabama's vote on delegates to the Democratic national convention in that year, and when he does this he is performing a service even though he knows that only a few score dedicated professionals like himself will ever have any desire to consult his findings. He is not going to produce a vibrant gem of literature, and it would be silly to say that he ought to.

Even so, that man is going to be a great deal better off if he understands that he is really on the fringe of literature. That is, he is writing something which, he believes, a few other people will some day read and profit by, and if he has any hope at all he must hope that the men who can understand what he is talking about will read him. To get through to these men, he needs some literary skill.

What do we mean when we talk about literary skill? In a vague sort of way, we mean the ability to write well; and the first and foremost of all of the skills that go to make up good writing is the ability to write clearly. Clarity of expression is what you must have to start with. Put on top of that any flourishes you like, you must begin with the ability to say what you mean in a way that other people can understand.

Now clarity of expression, which is at the basis of all literary achievement, depends on clarity of thinking. If you think clearly you may be able to write clearly; otherwise, not. And this is precisely the point that anyone who undertakes to write anything in the field of history needs to understand first of all. He is producing literature: which is to say that whatever he is dealing with he is first of all using words, and the words have to make sense. Whatever he says, he is obliged to say it so that someone else will know exactly what he is talking about; he needs to say it clearly, and in order to do that he needs to think it clearly.

It would be silly to repeat all of this except that there are fields in which the point is never grasped. If you have the heart for it, examine some day the things that are sometimes done in some of the social sciences. The knack of writing clearly seems to have been given up; a jargon has been invented, a special language which only the initiated can understand—and with it, I think, in far too many cases, comes a jargon of thinking. You no longer say what you want to say in plain, simple English. You rely on this particular vocabulary that has been devised for you; and I suggest that in far too many cases the reason you do this is that your own thoughts have gone beyond the bounds of ordinary intelligibility. You invent a sort of shorthand to convey your meaning, because when you do this you do not need to think things through; you can simply rely on clichés which have become acceptable through prolonged usage. You live in a landscape that is suffused by a pleasant haze, and instead of trying to dispel the haze you adjust yourself to it. What you write is finally taken seriously only by the people who talk your specialized language, because nobody else has any way to know what you are talking about. You have found a dialect that makes clear thinking unnecessary.

History has not yet reached that point. But its first defense has to be the realization that whatever one has to say must be said in terms that anyone can understand. Once we devote ourselves to taking in each other's washing we are on the downhill slope.

Unfortunately, this process of taking in each other's washing has begun to take hold in the field of history. If the profession has not devised its own special language it has tied itself up with some rather odd rules. The budding professor of history on any campus is under a powerful compulsion, imposed by the academic system, gathering greater force year by year. He must "publish"—which is to say that he must pursue his own scholarly investigation of something or other, reduce his findings to writing, and get them published in some medium which exists for the specific purpose of publishing such findings. The paper that comes out of all of this may have no great value to anybody in particular. It may indeed be something that no perceptive mortal will ever read except in the line of duty. The point is that there is no other way for the historian to prove his professional competence. If what he publishes finally turns out to be of lasting value, everybody is that much ahead of the game, but that point is incidental. At all costs he must publish. He cannot be a historian unless he is also a writer.

At first glance that seems all to the good. If we are interested in seeing history become literature, and if all historians are inexorably compelled to write, the simple law of averages ought to mean that an increasing amount of literature gets produced. Unfortunately, it does not work that way. For the young historian is under no compulsion whatever to write well. He simply has to have things in type, between covers, that show that he has collected, examined and commented on a proper number of shards and artifacts to pay for his ride up the escalator. It would be hard to imagine a system better devised to instill in him a positive distrust for good writing. The first thing he has to realize is that he is not writing for people concerned with literature. He is simply writing for other historians. He is supposed to be shedding light, but the light does not need to be very strong and the things it reveals do not need to be of any special importance. He simply has to show that he has gone into a dark place, struck a match, and looked about him. If he is devoted and studious, he may wind up as a footnote in some other man's book.

The field of history, of course, is extremely broad. If it

is to be cultivated properly an enormous amount of hard, unrewarding spadework has to be done. What I am complaining about here is the assumption that the spadework is all that matters; the attitude which holds that what is done here does not really concern anyone except the men who are in charge of the excavating. History becomes literature only when we force ourselves to realize that in the end the field is of importance chiefly because of the people who are not in it at all. Every so often someone has to come out of the field and say: "Look what I have found!"

In other words, history becomes important when it is told. As historians, of course we need to know what we are talking about, and we need to know how to say it intelligibly, but beyond that we need to know what history is *for*. Just what are we trying to get at here, anyway?

To begin with, we are trying to tell people what happened. We are the reporters for an age that is gone. The reporter has to begin by collecting his facts—he has to be extremely diligent at it, and if he scamps this part of his work he must very soon look for some other line of employment—but he also has to write his story so that other people may know what he knows. Furthermore, he may be as detached and objective as any man alive; but by the very nature of his work he must also be an interpreter; particularly when he is dealing, not with something that happened yesterday afternoon in the county courthouse, but with events that took place long before he himself was born. He is looking for the facts, but sometimes it is very hard to say what is fact and what is not, and it can be even harder to say which facts are meaningful and which are merely subsidiary. We have to pick and choose. Sooner or later we have to determine which data we build on and which we discard. As we do this we interpret the past in spite of ourselves.

The historian, in other words, draws the thing *as he sees it*, simply because it is not possible for him to do anything else. Try as he will to keep himself out of the picture, he is bound to get into it. The picture is his creation. He is the one who determines which facts are significant and which ones are not; in spite of himself, he winds up by saying what his chosen facts mean.

Take a brief example. In recent years there have been two excellent books on the famous Copperhead movement in the Middle West during the Civil War, each one written by an intelligent, competent, and dedicated professional historian. These men studied the same period, looked at the same evidence, did their level best to write solid factual accounts—and produced books which say diametrically opposite things. According to one book, the Copperhead movement was a deeply rooted affair that seriously threatened the fight to save the Union; according to the other book it was chiefly sound and fury, a thing of little substance that was inflated to unreal proportions by designing politicians.

This does not necessarily mean that one man was "right" and that the other man was "wrong." It simply means that each man was trying hard to follow the facts, and that neither man could see these facts quite as the other man did. To repeat, in each case the historian had to draw the thing as he saw it.

Now this, as Kipling pointed out, is precisely what the creative artist does. The historian, in other words, is in literature in spite of himself and there is no earthly way for him to keep out of it. And since this is the case—since history, once it advances one step beyond the paper for the learned journal, does become literature—it is up to the historian to see that it becomes good literature. The literary qualities of his work are central to what he is trying to do. Whether he knows it or not, he is finally impelled by the same force that drives the artist.

He is even, when you get right down to it, using the same materials. You remember Gibbon's remark that history in the end is simply a record of the crimes, the follies, and the misfortunes of mankind. What else is Hamlet?

Of course I am not trying to say that every man who writes history ought to look on himself as a budding Shakespeare. I do believe, however, that at its best history is more art than science. It must begin with the scientific approach, its own rigorous rules of evidence must be followed, it must not become an attempt to plead a cause or to twist the facts to fit some preconceived notion—but in the end it inevitably gives the reader the sort of thing the artist gives him: a view of life, an understanding, for good or for bad, of the world he lives in, an enlarged notion of what human beings are like, something of the vision that comes from the realization that these crimes, follies, and misfortunes that beset us arise from the struggle of finite man with an infinite fate. These things are inherent in the record itself. Try as he may to steer clear of them, the historian sheds light on them just because he is writing history.

So the historian's task presents a challenge. Once he goes beyond the point where he is simply providing building blocks for the use of other men in his own profession—once he addresses himself to the general reader—the historian has to face the fact that he is engaged in the literary art and that it is of very great importance for him to use the skills of that art. What he writes is finally going to have the effect of expanding his reader's horizon. It is going to move the reader emotionally, be the historian never so unemotional, just because a true account of man's unending struggle with destiny is always moving. To discharge his obligation fully—to meet the challenge which the writing of history presents—the historian must always bear in mind that he is for the moment acting as an artist, drawing the thing as he sees it for the God of things as they are.

Yet he is also discharging an obligation to history itself; or, to put it in another way, an obligation to society. As the world grows more and more complex, and as its complexities come to conceal an increasing number of pitfalls which can drop the whole human race straight down into the starless dark if they are not noticed in time, it becomes more and more important for men to understand their own history, to see how former trials were met, to learn how some of these pitfalls develop, and to get the knowledge they must have if they are to make their way through the perplexing and ominous twentieth century. Above all things, they need to know the story of their own past, and if they don't get it from the historian they won't get it from anybody—not, at least, in a form that will be of any use to them.

Thus the historian carries a massive burden. It would be lighter if we could just be sure that we know exactly what the story of the past really is, but we don't and we never can. All we can do is try to get it as straight as we can, knowing that at least part of the truth will elude us because it has gone missing somewhere. We can't find it, and if we could we probably wouldn't quite know what to do with it, so we have to put the story together according to the best light we have.

For all of us who have any connection with the field of history, it may be salutary to consider a few words written by a young man named Frank Haskell, who was an army officer from Wisconsin serving in the Army of the Potomac at the time of the battle of Gettysburg. Haskell was right in the middle of that fight—he was on Cemetery Ridge, by the little clump of trees, when Pickett's men came up there on the afternoon of July 3, 1863—and a few weeks after the battle he wrote his own account of it. The account did not satisfy him because it was incomplete: after all, he couldn't see everything, and he couldn't really be objective about what he had seen; he knew that some of the official reports were full of errors, and he did not trust the newspaper stories he had seen; and he concluded at last that a real, comprehensive account of this battle could never be written.

"By and by," he said, "out of the chaos of trash and

falsehood that the newspapers hold, out of the disjointed
mass of reports, out of the traditions and tales that come
down from the field, some eye that never saw the battle
will select, and some pen will write, what will be named
*the history*. With that the world will be, and if we are
alive we must be, content."

We are people who have some concern with history; if
we didn't we would not be here tonight. So we are the
people who have to look for the truth with the eyes that
never saw; the people who must comb through the chaos
of trash and falsehood, the disjointed reports and the uncertain traditions and tales, and try to make something
meaningful out of it all. Complete certainty is forever out
of our reach. If our work has any final value, that value
must depend very largely on our ability to see the essential
truth beyond the darkness and the error, and to create a
faithful picture out of something that never makes itself
explicit—on our ability, in short, to perform the historian's
difficult task not only with the historian's competence but
also with the skill, the insight, and the demanding conscience of the literary artist. In the end we can do no more
than draw the thing as we see it, knowing that we cannot
possibly see all of it. If we succeed, the history we write
takes its place as literature. Good history *is* literature.

# For an Emotional Understanding*

## June 1956

Very few facts of any real consequence still remain to be dug up about the American Civil War. History's secrets have been largely disclosed. We know about that war just about as much as our grandchildren will know, and the area of our knowledge today is not very much broader than it was a generation ago. Most of the returns are in, and they have long since been tabulated and analyzed.

Yet books about the war continue to be written, and since both authors and publishers work, very largely, in response to economic motivations, this can only mean that the American people still want to read such books. They want them, indeed, in a greater volume than at any time within living memory, and there is every indication that this desire will remain strong for a number of years to come. Which leads to the interesting question *why*.

It is easy enough to come up with stock answers—that this war was a prodigious experience, that almost everyone in America had a part in it, that our racial memory remains fascinated by the infinite drama and pathos of "the war between brothers," and that in this present era of uncer-

* *American Heritage* magazine, June 1956

tainty and doubt people look back to the supreme moment
of national crisis to see how we managed to get through
it and what lessons it may offer for people who have to
live in the modern world.

Yet all of those answers taken together are not quite
enough. They are perfectly correct, but when they are added
together something essential is lacking. The Civil War
story has been there all along, its salient facts all taped
and docketed, and the diligent students who have plowed
the field so thoroughly have left very little room for important new discoveries. The current spate of interest in the
war certainly does not depend on the writers' ability to
come up with hitherto undiscovered data; most emphat-
ically, it does not mean that the American public has
abruptly developed a fondness for reading an unending
rehash of an old familiar story.

What is going on now, clearly, is a deep and frequently
moving examination of the emotional significance of this
most profound of all our national experiences. We are not
yet wholly rational beings. We approach true understanding
through our emotions rather than through our intellects,
deplorable as that may be, and although we know about
all we need to know about the facts of the war we are
still feeling our way toward a comprehension of what those
facts mean.

For above and beyond everything else, the Civil War
was a matter of the emotions. It came about because men's
emotions ran away with them; it was borne, North and
South, for four mortal years because those emotions remained
strong; and its final significance, nowadays, is often more a
matter for the heart than the head. Except for the dedicated
student, nobody in particular cares to know more than is
already known about the inner whys and wherefores of
(to take a case at random) the great Battle of Gettysburg;
yet the man who can make us feel and see that stupendous

fight will get our attention because he helps us to comprehend the enormous intangibles which were involved there. Those intangibles, at Gettysburg and elsewhere throughout the Civil War story, reveal themselves most readily to the person whose feelings and imagination have been touched. Perhaps we ought to be able to reason our way to them, but most of us cannot. They come in moments of insight born of emotional understanding. There are many things about the Civil War which no historian can actually prove; he can only *show* them.

Which may help to explain why so much of the Civil War story nowadays is being told by the amateurs. With certain notable exceptions, the retelling which is going on is not the work of the established historians; it is being done very largely by the academically unsanctified. Whether this points to a shortcoming on the part of the established historians or to the chance that something may be wrong with the reading public is a separate question. The point is that what we are getting now is a useful, though at times a highly inexpert, re-examination of the Civil War which somehow reaches people who were not reached previously. It rarely gives us any facts that were not previously known; what it frequently does is help us to see things which were not formerly clear.

An excellent example is Mr. Earl Schenck Miers' new biography, *Robert E. Lee.** There already exist a great many studies of Lee. When Douglas Southall Freeman finished the monumental seven volumes devoted to Lee and Lee's lieutenants he left very little ground for later biographers to work, and for the reader who does not want Freeman's exhaustive detail there are plenty of excellent one-volume biographies of Lee. Yet Mr. Miers' brief book—it can hardly run to more than 60,000 words—is well worth having. It is not simply a reworking of familiar material. It

* *Robert E. Lee,* by Earl Schenck Miers. Alfred A. Knopf. 203 pp.

is a fresh look at Lee; an attempt to understand what the man was about, what moved him, and what his significance is in the story of the American people.

There are no surprises here; none are to be expected. Lee is, in this book as in all others, the genuinely great soldier, the man who in his own lifetime became a legend and always lived up to it, making the legend true. He was at his noblest, as Mr. Miers sees him, in the years after Appomattox, when he uncomplainingly threw himself into the task of helping the South back into its place in the Union. Few Americans have shown greater strength of character than Lee showed then.

Yet there was a limitation in the man—a singular inability to see and feel the main currents of his time. Disbelieving in secession and in slavery, he went to war to support both; he could never quite understand how Lincoln could turn slavery (in Mr. Miers' phrase) into "a weapon of moral fission" and maneuver the South into the position of opposing one of humanity's most basic aspirations. His Gettysburg campaign was doomed, not because the military cards were stacked against him, but because he understood in 1863 no better than he had understood in 1861 why the people of the North were really supporting Lincoln and the Union cause. In 1864 he and his army were brought to stalemate not so much by the superior resources of the North as by the fact that Lincoln had a vision which Lee never had—"a superb wholeness," as Mr. Miers puts it, "a broad, sweeping vision that had grasped the military, political, psychological and philosophical necessities of the great American conflict."

Here was the real tragedy of Lee. One of the great upward thrusts of the American spirit took place, and he never sensed it. The virtue of this little gem of a book is that it fully presents Lee's greatness but also brings this tragic shortcoming into high relief.

## Think Again

This re-examination of the Civil War, however, is not entirely a matter of emotional understanding. As David Donald points out, it is also a matter for the mental processes—for "rethinking," as he expresses it, for taking the enormous mass of data and looking it over carefully, for trying to determine (now that the jury has all of the important facts) just what the verdict ought to be.

Mr. Donald contributes immeasurably to this task in his new book, *Lincoln Reconsidered.** In this collection of essays he remarks that "the future is not likely to see major discoveries of new facts or fresh sources in the Civil War period"; what it does need is a fresh examination of the basic issues involved, a conscientious attempt to evaluate what is already known in the light of the new perspective which is ours simply because we come on the scene nearly a century after the shooting stopped.

What Mr. Donald is out to do—and very well he does it—is to take a fresh look at the whole Lincoln story in the light of modern scholarship and see what it all amounts to. He examines Lincoln from many angles—as political leader, as a figment of folklore, as military man, as the hero of emancipation—and he has a knack for expressing judgments that sound as fresh as if the whole subject were unexplored territory.

Best of all, he has the insight to realize that hard-and-fast judgments are not possible. Lincoln was one of the most complex and mysterious characters that America ever produced. His faults and virtues were strangely mixed, and sometimes what looks like a fault turns out to be a great source of strength. Lincoln was an opportunist, he drifted

* *Lincoln Reconsidered*, by David Donald. Alfred A. Knopf. 200 pp.

with the tide, he refused to be bound by doctrine or dogma, he handled each problem as it came to him—and if this sometimes drove his confreres almost to the point of madness, it was one of his chief elements of strength.

The popular picture of Lincoln is somewhat askew. We have been invited to look on him as the man who was hated by the politicians and loved by the people; yet there has not been in American history a cannier politician; the chance that was open to him to pose as the champion of the masses was simply missed, and Mr. Donald finds reason to doubt that in 1864 Lincoln held as tight a grip on the popular imagination as we usually suppose. What could have been done with the Lincoln myth, Mr. Donald suggests, by a modern publicity agent, is something to think about. He had everything—child of poor parents, born in a log cabin, a rail splitter and a painfully honest man, one who came up the hard way with no apparent advantages and everything against him—yet by modern standards almost no use was made of this in his political battles. Dipping his pen in acid, Mr. Donald muses: "The whole campaign, if managed by a Batten, Barton, Durstine and Osborn agent, should have been as appealing, as saccharine, as successful as the famous 1952 television appearance of our current Vice President."

Lincoln won neither the press, the politicians, nor the people; yet he was one of the most successful politicians in American history, he was the first President since Andrew Jackson to win re-election, and he got there (says Mr. Donald) primarily because he was a phenomenally successful operator of the political machine.

"Such a verdict," Mr. Donald admits, "at first seems almost preposterous, for one thinks of Lincoln's humility, so great as to cause his opponents to call him a 'Uriah Heep'; of his frankness, which brought him the epithet 'Honest Abe'; of his well-known aversion for what he termed the 'details of how we get along.' Lincoln carefully built up this public image of himself as a babe in the Washington Wilderness";

but he knew all the tricks, he played all of them in season and out of season, and in the end he won his chance to be a statesman by being a superb practical politician.

It is much the same, Mr. Donald believes, with the popular picture of the radical Republicans. They are usually cast as the villains of the Civil War drama. They obstructed Lincoln at every step, they thirsted for blood and vengeance, their devious schemes masked nothing much loftier than a desire for high tariffs and a clear field for the rising Northern industrialists, and altogether they were a bad lot, grasping and sly and conscienceless and, often enough, physically unattractive to boot. To this verdict Mr. Donald returns a simple "Nonsense." The radicals were very diverse people; they did not agree among themselves; they supported Lincoln more often than they combatted him; and as a general thing Lincoln knew exactly how to get along with them. "The Radical Republicans were only one of the many factions that pulled for control of the Lincoln administrations. Because they were noisy and conspicuous, their historical importance has been overstated. Beyond simple anti-slavery zeal, they held few ideas in common"—and, all in all, this writer suggests that it is time we thought more about them.

*Lincoln Reconsidered* is one of the most useful books in the Civil War field to appear in many years. It emphasizes a point of importance: that although we do have the facts about this period, we have not yet fully digested them, and we need to do a great deal more meditating before we arrive at final conclusions. Written with insight and a biting wit, this little book is a work of real significance.

## Mr. Lincoln's Weapons

Abraham Lincoln represented the frontier in many ways, not the least of which was the fact that he was an incurable tinkerer. Mechanical appliances fascinated him. The fron-

tiersman had so many chunks of hard manual labor to perform that any mechanical shortcut was bound to strike his
fancy: Lincoln had tried his own hand at inventing, and
the man with an interesting gadget to display could always
catch his interest.

As a war President, Lincoln had a wide-open chance to
indulge this interest. He was commander in chief of armies
engaged in the first of the modern wars, and most of the
authorities with whom he had to deal considered the old-
style muzzle-loader (for infantry and for field artillery alike)
wholly adequate. Perfectly practical breech-loading repeat-
ers were being made, and the mechanical revolution was
quite ready to extend the scope, intricacy, and general effectiveness of all the weapons the Army and Navy could
ask for; but except for Lincoln himself, hardly anybody in
Washington seemed to be interested.

As a result, Lincoln himself broadened the dimensions of
the presidency by becoming, in effect, his own Office of
Scientific Research and Development, not to mention his
own War Production Board. To him came inventors of high
and low degree, and if they could see no one else in the
government they could usually manage to see him. Fighting constantly against the inertia of a uniformed bureauc-
racy, Lincoln did his utmost to equip the Union armies
with up-to-date weapons.

This little-known aspect of Lincoln's presidency is inter-
estingly set forth by Mr. Robert V. Bruce in a stimulating
new book, *Lincoln and the Tools of War.** If Lincoln was a
brooding mystic he was also an eternal Yankee, and this
trait was not the least of his assets in his struggle to preserve the Union.

He gave to the army, for instance, breech-loading rifles.
(They were not universally used, by any means, but they
made their effect felt.) He pushed through a machine gun

* *Lincoln and the Tools of War,* by Robert V. Bruce, foreword by
Benjamin P. Thomas. The Bobbs-Merrill Co., Inc. 368 pp.

decades ahead of his time; if the army brass distrusted it and finally shelved it, it was nevertheless a perfectly good weapon—one which Lincoln could understand even if the generals could not. He experimented with rockets, explosives, submarines, mines; nearly lost his life, in fact, when a rocket blew up while he was watching a demonstration. Any citizen who entered the White House carrying a shiny new rifle was apt to be ushered into the President's office instead of being arrested by the secret service as a potential assassin.

Here, altogether, is a new glimpse at Lincoln; a completely fascinating one which adds immeasurably to one's understanding of what the great emancipator was up against in his White House years.

## The Other Extreme

From Lee and Lincoln to General Daniel E. Sickles is about as long a stride as one can take and still remain in the field of the Civil War. If Lee was nobility of spirit personified, Sickles was little better than an outright heel. A man of immense drive and energy, he was singularly lacking in principle. To him the whole immense conflict was little more than an opening by which a canny fellow on the make could pick up some good things for himself, and he went out picking with immense gusto and pertinacity.

In himself, Sickles was quite unimportant, although he was (at least in retrospect) an interesting sort of buzzard. His significance lies in the fact that he was a type. He exemplified perfectly the grasping, conscienceless operators who swarmed in on Washington during the war and did all that men could do to keep the deep moral issues underlying the conflict from becoming evident. If certain Southerners have felt that the whole Northern war effort represented nothing more than a scramble for riches and power, Sickles is one of the reasons.

Sickles gets the full treatment in *Sickles the Incredible*, by Swanberg.* This book shows him as a Tammany lawyer who was forever acquiring money, trouble, and notoriety in large quantities. His true character is perfectly illustrated by a sensational murder case in which he figured shortly before the war.

His wife had an affair with Philip Barton Key. Sickles found out about it and (himself one of the most flagrantly unfaithful husbands who ever lived) went into a great emotional tizzy. He made his wife give him a signed confession, went out and shot Key to death, won acquittal on the ground of temporary insanity—and by use of that written confession—and then calmly took his wife back into his home and resumed his domestic life quite as if nothing had happened.

When war came he opted for the Union, raised a brigade of infantry, and became a general. As a fighter he was valiant, though somewhat clumsy. He flouted Meade's orders at Gettysburg, put his troops into an unsound position and nearly lost the battle thereby—losing one of his own legs in the process. Then, afterward, by dint of pertinacity and immense political influence, he did his utmost to prove that his unwise move had been the height of tactical wisdom and that he had saved the Union cause. He managed to stir up such a fuss that the whole latter part of Meade's life was clouded by the controversy.

After the war he had further adventures. As military governor of the Carolinas during the Reconstruction era, he was tied in with one of the classic half-legendary wisecracks of American history. It was at a meeting over which Sickles presided that the governor of South Carolina turned to the governor of North Carolina and remarked: "There is a long time between drinks."

* *Sickles the Incredible*, by W. A. Swanberg. Charles Scribner's Sons. 423 pp.

Sickles found himself accidentally on the side of the angels at one time, playing a leading part in getting Jay Gould and Jim Fisk out of the Erie Railroad; then he became minister to Spain, muddling Spanish-American relations so thoroughly that it took a long time to get them untangled. In his old age he picked up the role of one-legged veteran and continued to push his tattered claims to the title of hero of Gettysburg. He did not die until 1914, a gusty, controversial old figure to the end.

Mr. Swanberg has given him an excellent biography, avoiding moral pronouncements and steering neatly away from the isn't-this-rascal-amusing flipness that is apt to creep into books of this kind. He lets the general's life and works speak for themselves.

## Let the People Know

The reporters who covered the war for Northern newspapers were an unusual lot. They came on the scene, really, before they were ready. The concept of the newspaperman as an unbiased chap who is simply trying to tell an accurate story of important events without regard for any other considerations had hardly begun to dawn on the journalistic profession in 1861; yet here, suddenly, was a tremendous convulsion which raised the public hunger for unadorned news to a height it had never reached before. The modern reporter overnight became a necessity. Since he did not then exist it was necessary to invent him, even though the inventors hardly realized what they were doing.

Emmet Crozier describes this process in *Yankee Reporters: 1861–1865*,* and contributes one of the best in the recent series of books which have been devoted to the subject. As a veteran newspaperman and a war correspondent of wide experience, Mr. Crozier is well fitted for the task. If, at

* *Yankee Reporters: 1861–65*, by Emmet Crozier. Oxford University Press. 441 pp.

times, he seems to feel that the Civil War reporters were always right and that the Union generals they had to contend with were always wrong, a brief glance at some of the generals involved makes the point of view understandable.

The war correspondent in the 1860s had an exceedingly tough job. The physical facilities for proper performance of his work were almost entirely lacking. The army had no idea of the importance of providing news for the people back home, although it could not exist unless those people understood what it was up to. Quite typical of the reaction of the higher brass was William Tecumseh Sherman's angry outburst. News? asked Sherman. Why, every soldier in the army wrote regular letters to the folks back home; that was all the news anybody needed. Sherman used to threaten to hang reporters, and once or twice he came tolerably close to carrying out the threats.

If the reporters had trouble with the generals, they also had trouble with themselves. They would gaily print news of immense value to the enemy, they would retail camp gossip by the column, and they were not above pronouncing judgment on the skill, patriotism, and intelligence of the generals about whom they wrote—especially if those generals had made things a little tough for them. They were woefully underpaid, many of them were excessively inaccurate in their reports, and all in all most of them fell far short of modern standards of reportorial competence.

But with all of their faults, they finally did an important job. Out of their work came the new idea of the place of the news reporter, an idea which is essential to the working of democracy. Out of it, too, came enlightenment for the American people.

## Desolate South

A good part of the South was a wasteland by the summer of 1865. Where the armies had gone there was outright physical devastation; where they had not gone there was the desolation due to the collapse of an economy and a social system. Across this wasteland, a few months after Appomattox, went a Yankee reporter to take notes on what he saw and to try to render a report on what the war had left.

The reporter may have been oddly chosen. He was John T. Trowbridge, an antislavery reporter, magazine writer and editor, who during the war had served neither in the army nor as a war correspondent but simply as a propagandist safe in New England. The ground he was to cover, the fighting that had furrowed it, and the people who lived upon it were all new to him. But he wrote, finally, a book which was substantially better than anyone had a right to expect. Edited by Gordon Carroll, this book has now been reissued under the title, *The Desolate South: 1865–1866,** and it is well worth reading.

Trowbridge seems to have begun by seeing what he expected to see. The battlefields themselves were monuments to Northern valor and Southern error. The recently freed Negroes were sober, hard-working, and orderly; the dispossessed Southerners who had so recently owned them were idle, ready to subsist on government handouts, unwilling and unable to make their own way and rebuild their shattered country. Everything, in short, fitted the preconceptions of a stout abolitionist who had never looked at any of this before.

But experience brought wisdom; furthermore Trowbridge was at bottom a first-rate reporter, a man of perception and understanding. Presently he found, in his editor's words, that he was "more concerned about the future welfare of a restored Union than he was in recounting the fears and terrors of a cruel war so recently won by the cause in which he believed."

As a result, this book—reduced to readable proportions

* *The Desolate South: 1865–1866,* by John T. Trowbridge, edited by Gordon Carrol. Duell, Sloan and Pearce-Little, Brown. 320 pp.

by skillful editing—stands as a memorable picture of what
the South looked like in the year immediately following the
war. Southerners had not yet had time to become "reconstructed"; they had hardly had time to realize what had
happened to them. Everything was in ferment, Union troops
still occupied the area, and to most people—black and white
alike—the mere task of getting enough to eat was all-en-
grossing. Trowbridge talked to everyone who would give
him a word (some Southerners, recognizing him as a Yankee,
gave him some tolerably hard words) and he wound up
with a story which was neither for nor against but simply
*about.*

Following Sherman's trail, he wrote factually and un-
emotionally about what Sherman's men had done. In Columbia, South Carolina—still pretty badly charred from Sherman's fire—he made no attempt to gloss over the behavior
of the Union soldiers. And he could find room for one salty
quote, from a South Carolinian speaking his mind about
Yankees: "They've left me just one inestimable privilege—
to hate 'em! I get up at half past four in the morning and
sit up till twelve at night to hate 'em."

# Morning Star[*]

## February 1958

According to the legend, America is a nation devoted to pure action—a muscular, highly organized country, as little given to brooding introspection and as dedicated to physical activity as a professional football team. The simile may be a good one; we see to it, by elaborate mechanisms, that our colleges and universities provide an adequate, unfailing supply of skilled athletes and worry very little if the output of thinkers—physicists, let us say, or other eggheads —runs a trifle short of the potential demand. It may be that we live up to the legend a little too ardently.

Yet the legend itself is somewhat out of date. We *are* an introspective people, and we are becoming more so every day. The current revival of interest in American history is an indication of the fact.

There are a great many reasons for that revival, but one of the strongest, certainly, is an instinctive desire to make a correct appraisal of our present status. That status grows out of all of the yesterdays which are history's especial concern, and it is obviously something we want to examine as closely as we can. What are we like, as a people? What sort

[*] *American Heritage* magazine, February 1958

of civilization have we finally built up here? What has become of us, at last, after all of these historic alarms and excursions? What does our society mean today, and where have we finally got to?

This, perhaps, is what we are really looking for, as we at last elevate history into something tolerably popular and familiar. The only trouble is that none of these plaintive questions can have a really satisfactory answer, because the simple truth is that we have not, so far, actually got anywhere yet—not anywhere that can serve as a place to pause and take a deep breath. History is a continuous process of change, and the change is still going on. We have not yet become something; we are still becoming. This bounteous year 1958 is no more the end of the journey than was 1861, or 1907, or any other year plucked at random from the calendar. New appraisals are all very well, but we Americans are still making our civilization, and what it will eventually look like is a secret.

So our introspection must be concerned chiefly with the attempt to get a line on that secret. We could hardly be better engaged, because even though we do not know just where we are going we are plainly going somewhere at a prodigious rate of speed, and unless we nourish a strong faith we are apt to wonder if the end of the journey may not be that steep place that leads down to the sea. To the examination of this secret Max Lerner applies himself diligently in a brooding, thoughtful new book aptly titled *America as a Civilization.**

We believe that we have a national tradition, says Mr. Lerner, but it is impossible to generalize about it very successfully because it is compounded of many subtraditions. We are the product of four separate waves of migration— the original movement of the Indians from Asia, the later movement of people from England and western Europe, the

---

* *America as a Civilization: Life and Thought in the United States Today,* by Max Lerner. Simon and Schuster. 1036 pp.

forced movement of the Negroes from Africa, and finally—
what Mr. Lerner calls "the polyglot ethnic strain"—the
great wave of all peoples from the Mediterranean, from central and eastern Europe, from Asia and from Latin America, and from everywhere else. Perhaps the one factor in
common with the greatest of these waves was the pervading
notion of America as a land of promise, a place where men
could find well-being and freedom. America, in short, was
built on a promise, and although we have been bothered ever
since about the degree to which that promise has been fulfilled, the significant thing as Mr. Lerner sees it is the fact
that the promise itself has always persisted. This is our
great "social myth"; it has always pulled us on, and it
always will, bringing abundant disillusionment but bringing
also recurring triumphs of advance and achievement.

Along with this dominant myth there is another fact which
Mr. Lerner considers unique to America. Alone among nations, he remarks, America has a history which "is also the
history of the three shaping forces of the modern Western
world"—industrialism as a technology, capitalism as a way
of organizing it, and democracy as a way of running both.
From these comes an immense dynamic force which moves
hand in hand with the great motif of promise. Whatever
we are becoming, then, it seems to Mr. Lerner highly likely
that future historians will look back on our American life
and see in it "one of the memorable civilizations of history."

All very well: and, specifically, how does this civilization
seem to be taking shape? Mr. Lerner does not try to give
any final, detailed answers; he simply looks about him, jots
down some of the memorable images that are fastening
themselves in our collective memories, and tries to arrive at
a few very broad conclusions. Significantly, he finds that,
even though we may be a less fluid people than we once
were, we have not yet developed a single, well-defined "rul-
ing class." We have an upper class, to be sure, a wealthy
class, perhaps even a dominant class, but we do retain social

mobility and the base of economic power is continually shifting. Rigidity has not yet set in.

Are we, with all of this, losing the drive and the sense of adventure that once (as we believe, anyway) character-ized America? We are still a dynamic society, but we are becoming very security-conscious. Are we torn by a clash between these two emotional states, with the old urge to make new beginnings conflicting with the urge to reach a safe spot where risks need not be taken? Possibly; for along with everything else Mr. Lerner concludes that "America is a happiness society even more than it is a freedom society or a power society." In our Declaration of Independence we asserted that one of man's inalienable rights is his right to pursue happiness, and we have been hard at the pursuit ever since, with varying degrees of success. Yet what else could come, in a land where the infinite promise of life is one of the traditional concepts? The pursuit of happiness is not a bad thing, once we understand just what happiness is and how it may best be attained.

We are no longer an isolated country, cut off from the rest of the world by broad oceans. Whether we like it or not, we are now one of the world's two great powers, and what we are and do—whether we are at our best or our worst—touches the imagination of the rest of mankind in a way (as Mr. Lerner suggests) that only one other society, the Roman Empire, ever touched it. The parallel is disquiet-ing, perhaps; for the Romans themselves lost their own im-agination, they came to value things more than they valued ideas, and the end was darkness. Will that be our destiny as a civilization? This grim question lies at the end of all our introspection.

To this question Mr. Lerner does not pretend to have a final answer. Any thoughtful student of American life can see many reasons for bleak pessimism, and as a highly per-ceptive man Mr. Lerner sees them as clearly as anyone needs to. But he retains his optimism—largely, it would seem, because our society is still in this process of becoming. The great enemy of any civilization, he suggests, is "the enemy within," which is simply rigidity. That has not yet come to us. We are still developing; our sources of creativeness have not gone dry. At the end of his long survey, Mr. Lerner is able to say, with Emerson: "We think our civilization is near its meridian, but we are yet only at the cock crowing and the morning star."

## Go It Alone

This exercise in considering our society as a world civilization is a useful one, but it does run counter to a powerful, deeply embedded impulse in American life—the impulse to look on America as a land set apart from all others, able to go its own way without reference to what the rest of the world may be doing. The man who is ruled by this impulse we call an isolationist, and when we try to appraise what we are and where we are going he is one of the people we need to examine. Who is he, and just how did he get that way?

An excellent study is now available in a book called *The Isolationist Impulse,** written by Selig Adler, professor of history at the University of Buffalo. Mr. Adler begins his inquiry by pointing out that it is necessary first of all to define isolationism correctly. American isolationism, he remarks, "has never meant total social, cultural, and economic self-sufficiency." Few Americans have ever believed in that, and the whole course of American history is against it. We have always exchanged both goods and ideas with the rest of the world, and we have never even dreamed of the iron-walled retreat into a hermit's life similar to that of the Japan of the shoguns. American isolationism is simply a determination to stay out of foreign wars, coupled with an un-

* *The Isolationist Impulse: Its Twentieth-Century Reaction,* by Selig Adler. Abelard-Schuman, Ltd. 538 pp.

wavering refusal to enter into alliances; a belief that we must always go it alone. Isolationists, says Mr. Adler, "cling tenaciously to faith in the unchangeability of our changing world."

This, to be sure, is where the shoe pinches, because the world is changing very radically, and some of the change comes from what we ourselves do. Yet the drive to go it alone is strong and it has deep roots in the American past, and Mr. Adler is concerned with getting these roots out and seeing what they amount to.

This inquiry leads him into a study of American history since, roughly, the time of the First World War. We got into a war which we had supposed we could stay out of, we oversold ourselves (once we got in) on what was going to be accomplished, and at the end it seemed that all of our fine hopes had been blighted. It was precisely then that the isolationist impulse came to full flower, and it proved an extremely hardy growth; bruised and trodden on though it has been of late, it is a long way from being dead. Where did it get its strength?

Step by step, Mr. Adler traces it. Woodrow Wilson ran into many difficulties, some of them self-created, when he came back from Paris with the draft Treaty of Versailles and the concept of a League of Nations. The liberals, previously among his strong supporters, fell away from him. The pro-league arguments were cast in an unreal, idealistic form, instead of being based on the obvious point that it was to our material interest to set up machinery that would curb aggression and war; and in 1919 America had grown very disillusioned about idealism. The election of 1920 was tragically misinterpreted; everyone assumed that it was a referendum on the treaty and on the league, when in fact (as Mr. Adler insists) it was the result of the interaction of many very complex forces, including simple war-weariness. Not for years thereafter would any political party be willing to go to the people with an internationalist program.

Then came the Harding Administration, in which, as Mr. Adler says, we tried to retain the benefits of isolationism and still reap the benefits of a privileged position in the world's market places. Washington washed its hands of responsibility for world economic conditions just when big business was getting into world economic affairs up to both elbows. Our statesmen and industrialists, imagining themselves perfectly in tune with each other, went in diametrically opposite directions.

The world economic depression—which, at least in part, grew out of this—greatly intensified the desire for isolation; and, as Mr. Adler says, "the isolationism of the 1930s was much more profound than the rather superficial detachment of the preceding decade." Dabbling in European affairs, apparently, had not only cost us our ideals but a great deal of money as well. We withdrew further into ourselves; at which moment came a new wave of aggressions, overseas, which tended to confirm our deep suspicions that international politics was no game for us. The New Deal did not stem the tide. On the contrary, the high-water mark of isolationism came in the neutrality legislation which bloomed between 1935 and 1937. Ironically, this legislation, Mr. Adler believes, made war all the more likely, for it helped persuade the megalomaniac Axis leaders that "the United States would stand by as they tore up the maps of Europe and Asia."

Out of all this came, at last, the Second World War, which reversed the trend. It was not followed by a general retreat of the liberals, as had been the case in 1919, and it clearly destroyed the isolationist argument that if we fought against Fascism we would destroy the very values we were trying to save. Also, on a purely material plane, it restored the pulsing prosperity which had been missing for more than a decade. We no longer wanted to get back to a happier prewar age, because the prewar age, this time, did not look worth regaining. There was an aftermath, to be sure, and the postwar witch hunts can be seen as a final flare-up of the isolationist mood, but the great drive was over.

Over—for keeps? Mr. Adler is not entirely certain. We have not yet found, he sagely remarks, an adequate substitute for isolationism. The collective security ideal is still in the blueprint stage, the international situation is (to say the least) unpromising, and there could still be a revival of the insular tradition. We have always been torn between a desire to use our power to stabilize the world and an urge to remain aloof. At the moment the internationalists seem to have won; but their victory, Mr. Adler warns, was "a decision rather than a knockout." The isolationists may yet demand a rematch; meanwhile, "the only certain thing about the future is its uncertainty."

## What We Are Like

Civilization, in the nature of things, is an experiment, and the test of its excellence (failing a better one) is probably its capacity for survival. The chief difference between our civilization and others may be that from the beginning ours has been a conscious experiment; at every step we have been pragmatists, shooting the works on the chance that what we were up to would somehow bring in the blue chips.

This, in any case, is the suggestion advanced by Bradford Smith in a light, entertaining, and frequently very perceptive book entitled *Why We Behave Like Americans.** In a way Mr. Smith (who was assisted in this book by Marion Collins Smith) is covering the same field Mr. Lerner plowed so assiduously; he is doing it with less gravity and in less space, and his book makes an excellent companion volume.

We have been trying new things in this country, says Mr. Smith, ever since the Pilgrim fathers were told by the Indians

* *Why We Behave Like Americans,* by Bradford Smith, assisted by Marion Collins Smith. The J. B. Lippincott Co. 322 pp.

that it would be a good idea to drop a rather dead fish in every corn hill to fertilize it, after which it would be every man for himself. The fathers tried it, it worked, and since then we have been receptive to new ideas, some of which panned out properly.

But although we know a great deal about ourselves, we do not necessarily understand too much; and Mr. Smith's book is an essay directed toward a broader understanding. Understanding, he believes, grows out of a knowledge of all of the things that go to shape a culture—physical environment, human influences, institutions, artistic expressions, and the way in which the people involved go about making a living, reproducing their kind, and expressing their inner yearnings. His book, accordingly, is directed (without too much solemnity) toward an examination of all of these aspects of American society, and it is highly readable.

There are, as Kipling once remarked, many different ways of constructing tribal lays, and all of them are right. Mr. Lerner's way is solemn and thorough; Mr. Smith's is light and occasionally irreverent. As a sample, in his discussion of the American character, he expresses himself thus:

"Americans are a peculiar people. They work like mad, then give away much of what they earn. They play until they are exhausted, and call this a vacation. They love to think of themselves as tough-minded businessmen, yet they are push-overs for any hard-luck story. They have the biggest of nearly everything including government, motor cars and debts, yet they are afraid of bigness. They are always trying to chip away at big government, big business, big unions, big influence. They like to think of themselves as little people, average men, and they would like to cut everything down to their own size. Yet they boast of their tall buildings, high mountains, long rivers, big meals. Theirs is the best family, the best neighborhood, the best state, the best country, the best world, the best heaven. They also have

the most traffic deaths, the most waste, the most racketeer-
ing."

Well, so far, so good; and it is fairly easy to go on in this
vein, so long as you are not required to touch base anywhere.
Mr. Smith does touch base; that is, he can think hard while
writing easily (not too simple a trick), and he does a really
good job of describing the way in which the American spirit
expresses itself. It does so, he seems to feel, on a largely
informal basis. Every crisis in American history finds people
doing some of their biggest jobs through wholly voluntary
associations—as via the Sons of Liberty, in the days when
a great ferment of libertarian ideas was leading up to the
American Revolution; as in the case of the Underground
Railroad, which did so much to put the skids under slavery.
The point is that Americans always want to remain free
private citizens and individuals, but they do realize that
they are bound to the community and must exert their
influence upon it. They advance democracy not so much
through politics as through an *ad hoc* system of working
together on their own hook. We are rugged individualists,
but we always recognize that we belong to the group.

So Mr. Smith goes on, sketching in briefly all manner of
facets of American life, from public schools to newspapers
and from political caucuses to trade associations and the
conventions of fraternal organizations. He comes to no more
positive final conclusions than Mr. Lerner reaches; like him,
he does manage to complete his survey with a feeling of
hope—the result of an appraisal of a society which draws
vitality and optimism from its youth and its abundance. And
like him, too, he has the sense of a nation which has not
yet "arrived" but which is still working its way—blindly, and
often with great waste and error, but always with energy—
through its perplexing but promising formative stages.

# Aristotle and Pandora*

## August 1959

When the Spanish and Portuguese explorers of the late fifteenth and early sixteenth centuries broke though the established horizons and compelled their fellows to get acquainted
with the unknown, they turned the medieval mind loose in
a world of fantasies and marvels. New myths were created
and old myths regained credence. Columbus suspected that
he had found either Japan or the true terrestrial paradise;
the flat Florida peninsula was believed to contain the authentic Fountain of Youth; the Seven Enchanted Cities of ancient
legend were thought to lie, attainable at last, somewhere
north of Mexico; and such creatures as dragons, griffins,
unicorns, sea monsters, giants, and headless men with eyes
in their chests were accepted as realities in the fabulous
lands beyond the seas. Men who supposed that they had a
fairly complete understanding of an orderly cosmos found
themselves living in a world where almost anything might
be true.

In such a world, men have to recast many of their ideas,
and out of the intellectual ferment that developed in the
sixteenth century came notions which have immense rele-
vance to the state of today's world. For the age of discovery

* *American Heritage* magazine, August 1959

took the lid off of the world, a process not entirely unlike the opening of Pandora's box; some of the ideas that came out when the lid came off have had an amazing development and have become very hard to live with, and constitute present-day problems of the first magnitude.

Among these, apparently, must be listed that enormous obstacle to peace and good will, race prejudice itself; and a succinct and provocative discussion of the development of this problem is provided by Lewis Hanke in his compact little book, *Aristotle and the American Indians,*\* which is subtitled: "A Study in Race Prejudice in the Modern World."

As Professor Hanke makes clear, true race prejudice hardly existed in the fifteenth century. Mankind then was divided into two antagonistic groups, to be sure, but the division was between Christians and infidels rather than between men whose skins had different pigmentation. It was only when Europeans entered not only the Americas but Africa and Asia as well that the issue of race became dominant.

It developed naturally enough. The new lands that were being opened had enormous wealth. The men who occupied these lands were either uncouth barbarians or, at the least, eminently conquerable, and in any case they were strange folk of a different race. Who were they? How should they be treated? Could they be Christianized and civilized? Was it not, perhaps, wholly right and proper for Europeans to conquer and despoil them by force of arms?

The debate that centered around this final question was carried on most extensively in Spain, which was making the largest conquests and which was also an extremely devout nation, troubled by pangs of conscience. In 1550 Charles V took the remarkable step of ordering all further conquests suspended until a special assembly of theologians and counselors could debate the matter. In his examination of the ensuing debate Professor Hanke centers his attention

---

\* *Aristotle and the American Indians,* by Lewis Hanke. Henry Regnery Co. 164 pp.

chiefly on two distinguished opponents—the Dominican friar Bartolomé de Las Casas, who argued that the Indians had natural rights which had to be respected, and the famous Renaissance scholar Juan Ginés de Sepúlveda, who held that the Indians were such crude and brutish people that their subjugation was lawful.

Given the circumstances, it was probably inevitable that Sepúlveda's idea should prevail, inasmuch as the pressure for continued conquest and exploitation was all but irresistible. But it was the justification which Sepúlveda offered that did the damage. For Sepúlveda brought forward the ancient theory of Aristotle—that a part of mankind is set aside by nature to be slaves in the service of a master race. The Indians, obviously, were the sort of inferior folk Aristotle had in mind.

As Professor Hanke points out, the debate led to no formal, clear-cut decision, and the Spanish Crown actually made sincere attempts to follow the humane doctrine of Las Casas. But the Aristotelian notion took hold. It was mightily comforting, not only to Spaniards but to all other Europeans who could see huge profits coming from the merciless exploitation of less fortunate peoples. If these people of another race were, in fact, ordained by natural law to serve their betters, and if you as a conqueror could elect yourself as one of the betters—well, what more could the master race ask?

It could ask for nothing more, and the notion has prevailed ever since. It did not always need Aristotle, as a matter of fact. Professor Hanke calls attention to the fact that the Protestant English embraced the idea, and cites the possibly apocryphal tale of the New England assembly which, in 1640 or thereabouts, considered three resolutions:

"1. The earth is the Lord's and the fullness thereof. Voted.

"2. The Lord may give the earth or any part of it to his chosen people. Voted.

"3. We are his chosen people. Voted."

So it went, and so the people of Europe adapted themselves to the idea that other races were somehow set aside
by nature to be subject folk. It was a very reassuring notion
indeed, for those who believed themselves to be on top of
the heap, and the idea took hold and grew. Las Casas might
go on insisting that "all the peoples of the world are men"
and that men have natural rights which cannot be overborne;
the infinite weight of the people who could wax rich and
prosperous by following Aristotle was too great for him,
and one of the great tragedies of world history was the
fact that just as the white Europeans entered on a period
of closer and closer contact with non-white races, they developed a powerful conviction of their own innate superiority. You can justify any imaginable oppression or injustice if
you can first demonstrate that the people you are oppress-
ing were ordained by natural law to be your servants. The
records of the Nuremberg trials contain hair-raising testimony about the things men will feel free to do when they
follow Aristotle's theory.

So the controversy of the 1550s still goes on, and we
have not left Aristotle behind us. There may, however, be
a way out, which Las Casas probably would have understood. Professor Hanke quotes the Mexican José Vasconcelos,
who was asked how he proposed to solve the Indian problem; had he considered the means by which the Indians
should be educated? Vasconcelos replied: "No—we are
simply going to treat them like human beings, with Christian
principles."


## The Basis for Slavery

The belief in racial inequality has been fairly expensive,
considering the lives that have been spent because of it. Out
of it we got, among other things, the institution of chattel
slavery in the United States. Slavery is gone, but we fought

a four-year war to make it go, and now and then it occurs
to us that the war somehow grew out of the belief that there
are in this world, by an unalterable law of nature, a master
race and a subject race.

Negro slavery and its part in bringing about the American
Civil War have been studied, questioned, and hashed over
for the better part of a century, and the whole business has
suffered just a little because it has been sicklied o'er by the
pale cast of what now and then passes for thought. The war
was fought because many things had gone wrong, and it is
easy enough now for studious men to examine trends, social and economic developments, and the hidden intricacies
of roughhewn American politics and conclude that the whole
war was a tragic mistake that could easily have been avoided
if the men of the 1860s had only managed to have the
benefit of the serene wisdom which their grandchildren were
able to attain three-quarters of a century later. This is quite
possibly true: and yet the point does remain that the war
somehow had its beginning in the simple fact that one race
held another race in slavery, and beyond that there lies the
fact that the owning race considered itself infinitely superior
to the race that was owned.

This was a rather expensive attitude, since it led to the
loss of some 600,000 lives. If today we are paying rather
more attention to the approaching centennial of the Civil
War than the situation really seems to warrant, the trouble
probably comes from this business of the race problem,
which Aristotle helped bequeath to us.

And the race problem does date back to the notion that
there are inferior and master races on this earth. For several
years, a classic discussion of this matter has been Dwight
Dumond's *Antislavery Origins of the Civil War in the United
States.** This is now available in a paperback reprint from

* *Antislavery Origins of the Civil War in the United States*, by Dwight
Lowell Dumond, with a foreword by Arthur Schlesinger, Jr. The University
of Michigan Press. 133 pp.

the University of Michigan Press, and it is a book of peculiar timeliness today.

From the beginning we had slavery in the United States, and from the beginning this fact pressed heavily on the national conscience. This conscience was quieted, for a long time, by a number of factors, among them the tragic fact that even the people who did not believe in slavery did, for the most part, believe in the inequality of the races. One race was inferior to the other, as Aristotle had said; set it free and you would create a completely insoluble problem—equality between basically unequal races. No one was quite ready to look such a development in the eye, so antislavery agitation in this country began by demanding a system of colonization.

In the course of time—say by the middle 1830s—men who considered slavery an unendurable wrong began to see that colonization was not quite the answer. Slavery infringed on the idea of freedom, and that idea is one which has to be taken straight; it runs all across the board, or it is phony. So either slavery or liberty would eventually have to go, and the antislavery movement could no longer base itself on colonization, or on any other adjustment to the notion that there is an unbridgeable gap between the races. The story of the antislavery movement in the 25 years preceding the Civil War is very largely the story of the effort to put this point across. Freedom and abolitionism were on the defensive in 1834, but slavery was on the defensive by 1860. Public opinion, in the North, swung over to a new orientation.

Mr. Dumond does not hold to the traditional belief that it was mostly New England that led the way to this new viewpoint. The thing was settled in the great Mississippi Valley, as he sees it; if the old Southwest was the great stronghold of slavery, the old Northwest was the area in which the antislavery decision was finally reached, and "had the region east of the mountains somehow been blotted out in 1830 and these two western regions been an entity unto themselves, things would not have happened very much differently from what they did. . . ." The hard determination to abolish the evil came out of what we now call the Middle West, as Mr. Dumond interprets the matter; and the South viewed things correctly when it saw Lincoln's election in 1860 as a final, fatal threat to the continued existence of the peculiar institution.

For Lincoln, besides being a personal opponent of slavery as an institution, had a radically new notion about the nature of the federal government. While he was on his way from Springfield to Washington he said, in effect, that the states were really political subdivisions of the United States, and bore about the same relation to the nation that a county bore to a state. In his inaugural address, "he enunciated a political philosophy designed to make the mandates of an unrestrained numerical majority the operative law—it was a complete endorsement of the doctrine of the higher law." The Republican victory in 1860 was essentially a victory for the higher law doctrine, and this meant that the governmental machinery, which previously had protected slavery, would no longer be adequate.

## Who Is Superior?

For slavery was a holdover from the old colonial era, and in the increasingly mechanized, highly organized world of the mid-nineteenth century it could survive only by mutual consent. As Mr. Dumond remarks, "Few . . . institutions were ever so dependent as slavery upon tranquillity." When the guns opened on Fort Sumter, America's tranquillity was violently shattered, and the conditions under which slavery could live no longer existed. Perhaps the real depth of the tragedy which followed lies in the fact that the nation destroyed slavery without first discarding the belief in racial inequality.

In the violent convulsion of the Civil War, it is significant that the hard blows were struck not so much by the dedicated abolitionists as by the military and industrial technicians who brought the North's overwhelming strength to bear on the Confederacy's basic weaknesses. One of these—a man who had a far larger part in the final Union victory than he usually gets credit for—was the devoted, hard-working quartermaster general of the Union Army, Major General Montgomery C. Meigs, whose biography is presented by Russell F. Weigley in an excellent study, *Quartermaster General of the Union Army.**

A career soldier and an engineer officer of distinction, Meigs had one of the key roles in the Northern war effort. It was up to him to outfit and equip the Union armies: shoes, wagons, tents, steamboats, uniforms, horses, mules, hospital equipment, railroad rails, pontoon bridges—the all but infinite list of things the Union armies needed was made up, bought, and distributed under Meigs's direction, and during the war he was responsible for the spending of more than $675,000,000. All things considered, he performed his job with remarkable efficiency. Toward the end of the war the job actually looked like simple routine.

In effect, it was Meigs's task to take the enormous potential material strength of the North and transform it into actual strength that could be applied on the battlefield. In doing this he had to make certain not only that the stuff was produced but that it was distributed to the places where it was needed, and it was here that Meigs did his best work. As the war progressed, the Confederate services of supply progressively collapsed; those of the Union continued to improve, and the striking contrast between the condition of the two armies on the Petersburg front at the

* *Quartermaster General of the Union Army*, by Russell F. Weigley. Columbia University Press. 396 pp.

end of 1864 is profoundly significant. The Northern states not only had much the greater resources to draw on, but they did a far more effective job of using what they had.

Meigs was an odd mixture. As Mr. Weigley emphasizes, he was in many ways a man of the new day, "of the materialistic, mechanically and scientifically inclined America born in the second half of the century of industrialization, urbanization, and technological change"; but at the same time he was a dedicated sort of person, convinced that slavery was a profound moral wrong, almost mystically devoted to a vision of himself as an instrument in "the consummation of some inscrutable but certainly glorious divine purpose." He saw the war as a sort of penance which the nation had to undergo for the sin of having permitted slavery to exist in the first place, and he never doubted that victory had resolved a great moral issue.

But a belief of this kind can be a dangerous possession; for unless it is linked with deep compassion and a great breadth of understanding it can be—and in Meigs's case, actually was—the source of hatred and bitterness. When the war ended, Meigs had little room in his heart for reconciliation with the beaten foe. One of his friends from the prewar professional army was Gustavus W. Smith, who became a major general in the Confederate Army. Shortly after the war Smith was in Washington and tried to renew the old friendship with Meigs. Meigs would have none of him, and in his diary he wrote bitterly: "I for one have no pleasure in association with such as he. Hemp or salt water should be offered to all such had I the power." He complained repeatedly that the Southerners, owning themselves beaten, did not feel at all repentant; to him they were sinners, and he wanted them to confess their sins and ask for absolution. He came to believe, at last, that the men of the South would not believe they were wrong until a dozen or more of their leaders had been hanged.

To the eternal good fortune of this nation, a milder point

of view at last prevailed, and the hangings Meigs wished to see did not take place. And the fact that a basically decent man like Meigs could come to feel as he felt illustrates in a striking way the evils that arise when human beings permit themselves to believe that they are somehow better men than other people are.

For Meigs, and the other vengeful Northerners who felt as he did, had simply fallen into the old error: they had become convinced of their own innate superiority to a large segment of their fellow citizens. In a queer, upside-down way they were serving the old fallacy, following not so much Aristotle as the Pharisee who publicly thanked God that he was not as other men were. If there is a moral in all of this it perhaps is that any sort of belief in group superiority is the source of evil.

Slavery had been born, and had developed to the point where the country had to fight a ruinous war to get rid of it, because men had taken for granted the notion that one race of men is inherently better than another race. Slavery itself may indeed have been a great moral wrong, but it existed not because some men were sinners but simply because all men had given way to a delusion about fixed grades and classifications in the great family of man. Failing to understand that it was race prejudice itself rather than willful human wickedness that was at the bottom of the nation's troubles, the Northerners who clamored for hangings and proscription lists were doing no more than perpetuating the real evil. Any belief that justifies the conqueror in doing whatever he chooses to do to the conquered is bound to be the source of profound wrong.

The lesson is there for us, if we have the wit to learn it. Considering the state of the world today and the hazards that it presents, it is perhaps high time that we got on with our studies.

# Setting the Pattern[*]

## June 1961

The first half of the nineteenth century in America sometimes appears to have been little more than an eventful and
confusing prelude to the great trial by fire which was to be
the American Civil War. It began with the first bright triumph of Jeffersonian democracy, and it ended with the
development of sectional feelings so intense that the country
narrowly escaped being fragmented; here perhaps was
simply a time of preparation, in which nothing had been
finally settled, a time that could do no more than germinate
a conflict whose outcome could not be foretold. America
was still in a process of becoming, not yet sure that it was
a nation or that it could develop a genuinely national significance.

Yet some sort of pattern was being set. The familiar statement that the country would ultimately be shaped by its
"continental destiny" may be nothing more than a half-
mystical catch phrase born out of later knowledge, but something was working. By the time of the Mexican War the
weight of the future was exerting its effect; the storied lost
cause was possibly lost more than a decade before it was
born.

[*] *American Heritage* magazine, June 1961

This, in any case, is the judgment of Charles M. Wiltse, a man well qualified to have an opinion on the matter. As the distinguished biographer of John C. Calhoun, Mr. Wiltse has studied this period in much detail and with a discerning eye; and in his most recent book, *The New Nation,** he argues that between 1800 and 1845 America did in fact attain nationhood. The Civil War, at frightful cost, merely ratified a decision that had already been made.

When the century began, nothing had been settled. The ordinary American in 1800, as Mr. Wiltse says, was "proud of his country but not quite sure whether his country was the United States or only that one of them in which he happened to live." The end of the strange and apparently pointless War of 1812 did indeed leave most Americans feeling that at last they were on their way, but nobody was quite sure where they might actually be going. Aaron Burr, General James Wilkinson, and the Essex Junto had shown that the paths might be various and divergent. The exuberant nationalism of the immediate postwar years gave way, in less than a decade, to intense contention.

The debate over the Missouri Compromise in 1820 brought this contention to a head. It was the permanence of the Union itself that was at stake here; the cultural and economic division between slave-state South and free-state North had already become of critical importance. Even this early, as Mr. Wiltse sees it, the South had developed "a social and political unity that could not tolerate change"; at the same time the free states, caught up by industrial growth, were becoming more and more diversified and hence more and more committed to change. The South bore the burden of slavery, which Mr. Wiltse aptly calls "the costliest and least efficient labor system ever devised by the wit of man for his own degradation"; yet any attack on this system had to appear, to Southerners, as a threat to Southern pros-

---

* *The New Nation: 1800–1845,* by Charles M. Wiltse; edited, with a foreword, by David Donald. Hill & Wang. 237 pp.

perity and freedom; and in a truly unified nation slavery must cease to be merely a local institution and must instead be everyone's responsibility.

Sectional strife and sectional compromise, accordingly, marked the coming decades. By one expedient and another, the breaking point was staved off, and an uneasy balance was maintained. Yet the balance was forever tilting against the Southern section. Wedded to the belief that the slave system was permanent, the South became more and more static; but elsewhere there was an intense and increasing dynamism, born of the rush to occupy western lands, of the accelerating pace of industrial development, and of the spirit of the age itself. The dynamism was bound to win. Mr. Wiltse writes:

> The truth was that the United States of the nineteenth century was in many respects a forerunner of the great powers of the modern era—a nation occupying a vast territory, with a heterogeneous economy in which measures helpful to one interest might well be hurtful to another. France and Britain still relied on the exploitation of alien peoples in colonial empires; Spain and Russia were still sunk in feudalism; Germany and Italy had not yet been born. Only in America was the typical economy of the twentieth century being worked out, with all the false starts, mistakes, and growing pains that are the normal lot of the pioneer. Had it not been for the moral issue raised by the existence of slavery, American sectionalism would undoubtedly have worked itself out earlier than it did.

By 1846 this struggle could go only one way. Slavery was going down the drain, no matter what anybody might do about it. The irrepressible conflict might by this time have become genuinely irrepressible, but its end was foredestined.

The balance of power lay with those who believed that the United States was one nation, and nothing the Southern section could do would restore the old equilibrium. In 1846 the South was about to make its great strike—the war with Mexico, to result in the acquisition of Texas, the empty plains to the west, and the California empire on the edge of the sunset. Texas would become a slave state, but it would be balanced by Oregon, overbalanced by California, and eventually doomed by the broadened horizon which could be reached only by a whole country.

Mr. Wiltse sums it up very well:

> The dogma of state sovereignty had been kept alive, in spite of the nationalistic forces released by the second war with Britain, by the urgent need of a substantial agricultural interest to protect itself against a more profitable and more aggressive industrialism. The slave-based nature of the agricultural interest gave a moral character to the industrial challenge, but the contest did not differ in essence from the upheavals then beginning in Europe out of which would come the end of serfdom, and untimately the concept of a balanced economy in which subsidies—to agriculture as well as to industry— would be freely used as instruments of policy. . . . The kind of particularism represented by states rights became obsolete when the advance of the industrial revolution concentrated physical power at the only governmental level with resources adequate to support the new technology, and enough disinterestedness to seek reconciliation of conflicting interests.

By the middle of the 1840s this point had been reached. There would be just one country between Canada and the Rio Grande. A few years later, 600,000 young men would have to die to prove this fact, but the fact itself had already taken shape.

## Conflict for Power

What had been going on through all of this, however, was more than just a conflict between opposing ways of looking at the kind of nationality that was to develop in America. The demand for states' rights might, and did, lead at last to an attempt to break the nation into its component parts; but now it is clear that it really represented a determination on the part of the Southern economy to maintain control over the federal government. The opposing force, which tried to strengthen the central government at the expense of state authority, was trying to end that control and put the reins in different hands. Basically, here was a struggle for power.

Roy Nichols sees it that way, and he enlarges on this thesis in *The Stakes of Power,*\* a cogent book which makes an excellent companion piece to Mr. Wiltse's book. (As a matter of fact, the two books are meant to go together. Edited and given brief forewords by David Donald, they are the first two in a series of six which will have the general heading, The Making of America.)

Implicit in Mr. Nichols' argument is the interesting implication that the permanence of the single nation was subconsciously taken for granted even when the danger of a division was greatest. The Northern and Southern sections had developed economic and social systems with profoundly different requirements. To satisfy those requirements, the leader of each section had to have power in Washington. Throughout the stormy 1850s, the South held that power almost completely. There were Northern presidents, but they had been nominated by conventions under Southern control. Cabinets were led by Southerners, and so was most

---

\* *The Stakes of Power: 1845–1877,* by Roy F. Nichols; edited, with a foreword, by David Donald. Hill & Wang. 246 pp.

of the legislative and judicial machinery. What made the crisis of 1860 so dangerous was the increasing frustration of the North over its inability to assert control and the rising apprehension of the South because of the likelihood that the Northern bid for power could not be staved off much longer.

Out of this came not only the Civil War itself but the internal struggle which racked the federal government—and ultimately affected the destiny of the entire nation—while the war itself was in progress. As Mr. Nichols emphasizes, Lincoln was so anxious to preserve the Union (which he saw as the symbol of an all-important experiment in democracy) that he was willing to permit slavery to continue to exist if necessary; but the zealots in his party wanted above all to destroy the political power of the South, which was based on slavery, and the act of secession simply intensified the conflict in Washington. Here Lincoln outmaneuvered his antagonists. He put through his own definition of war aims, kept his political forces intact, and showed that he was quite likely to direct the reconstruction which would follow victory.

Lincoln saw the underlying reality very clearly. When the struggle for power erupted into actual war, the whole situation became fluid; he could not direct the war intelligently without keeping the postwar program always in mind. The war would be followed by a reconstruction, but not by a restoration.

Meanwhile, the economic necessities of the North were finding their outlet. An economic rebuilding of the nation took place in the midst of the war. The subsidy legislation demanded by Northern interests, unattainable as long as Southerners held power in Washington, was put through while the armies were still fighting—a new banking system, distribution of public lands, aid to western settlement and to European immigration, transcontinental railroads, tariff protection. Mr. Nichols describes it in these words:

. . . this economic legislation constituted a giant reconstruction project. On the eve of these enactments the
United States had been a laissez-faire, individual-enter-
prise state. It was now transformed into a nation with
grand ideas of Federal subsidy, encouragement and protection to corporate enterprise. These grants and sub-
sidies, added to the giant war expenditures, were to
stimulate the national economy to take great strides in
the mobilization and accumulation of wealth.

The struggle for power, of course, did not end when the
war ended, which is why Mr. Nichols carries his book
through to 1877 instead of stopping at 1865. That odd chain
of events which is spoken of as "reconstruction" involved
reconstruction of the nation, not just of the South. Andrew
Johnson proved unable to wield the power that Lincoln had
exercised. The party zealots took it away from him. The
Southern states were transformed, not merely because car-
petbag governments indulged in riotous extravagance and
created an immense burden of debt, but also because their
social and economic functions were permanently broadened.
The landed elite had lost control, and the idea of state
responsibility for education and welfare was introduced into
the South.

Hand in hand with this went a similar transformation in
the North, and as Mr. Nichols remarks, "a large degree of
power was in process of transfer from the government to
the leaders of the growing business world." In the North as
well as in the South this was accompanied by distressing
scenes of corruption and waste. The redistribution of power,
creating first a new political power and second a non-polit-
ical power which controlled the dominant party organization,
kept on working; and finally, as the unhappy Grant administration drew toward a close, a popular revolt began against
the generally corrupt alliance between these two powers.
The broad compromise which accompanied the advent of

the Hayes administration was the symbol of this revolt. Business elements remained dominant, but at least a measure of political influence returned to the reconstructed South.

What, altogether, had been going on? Mr. Nichols puts it this way:

> For more than twenty years the American nation had been in the throes of changing its political leadership. In the mid-forties, the Democratic party, dominated by its Southern leaders, had been in control. This party wanted government to be strong and rambunctious in foreign affairs, truculent toward European powers. But at home it prescribed a policy of inaction, of hands off. Little was to be undertaken and a minimum spent. Such a government, however, was not in step with the times. The great continent and the restless mobile population produced a combination of forces which dictated action, and any government which refused to respond was doomed. The Democratic party under Southern domination felt itself firmly enough established to defy the spirit of the times. The result was disastrous.

Yet the realignment, which resulted in a fearfully expensive war, was not permanent. The end of the reconstruction era "left the issue of who was to control still undetermined." Never since has there been a new power with greater strength than the one which held sway during the pre-Civil War generation. The elements which contested for such high stakes in the war and postwar years are still present. Politics today still reflects the power struggle.

## The Ultimate Destiny

These, of course, are backward glances; things seen from the long perspective, when the dominant forces at work

underneath day-to-day crosscurrents and turbulences at last
become clear. It is interesting to turn back to see how matters
looked, to a foreign observer, at the moment when things
were still in a state of flux and when the nation was still
groping uncertainly to lay hold on its destiny. How would
an outsider see the chaotic United States of the 1850s?

Philip Schaff was a young German theologian who was
dispatched to Pennsylvania in 1844 by the German Reformed
Church in response to a plea from the Pennsylvania Synod
of that church, which wanted an accredited and learned
"Doktor" to teach historical and exegetical theology in a
budding backwoods seminary at Mercersburg, Pennsylvania.
To the orderly German mind of that day America looked
like an utter wilderness of confused and conflicting religious
sects, and one of Schaff's colleagues, baffled in the attempt
to understand what was going on, cried out: "God forgive
Christopher Columbus for having discovered America!" But
Schaff came to America, taught at Mercersburg and later
at Union Theological Seminary, and established himself as
one of the greatest of ecclesiastical historians.

In 1854 he revisited Berlin and there delivered lectures
on the state of things in America. These were subsequently
made into a book, which is now being reprinted with editing and an introduction by Perry Miller—*America: A
Sketch of Its Political, Social and Religious Character**—and
this book shows how a German scholar appraised America
at the moment when the nation was stumbling forward to
its moment of greatest crisis.

Much of the book deals with the contentions, differentia-
tion, and activities of the various religious denominations in
the America of that day and is naturally of interest only
to a specialized audience. But Schaff's size-up of the strange
new society of which he had become a part is still worth

* *America: A Sketch of Its Political, Social and Religious Character,* by
Philip Schaff; edited, with an introduction, by Perry Miller. The Belknap
Press of Harvard University Press. 241 pp.

reading; for he could see something prodigious taking shape underneath the conflict of voices and of interests, and he believed that what he saw was nothing less than the development of a vital force which would provide the world with leadership.

America in 1854 struck him as "a wonderful mixture of all nations under heaven." To tour America was to tour the world; here was everybody, "an ethnographic panorama," with a new character somehow emerging from a fusion of the most diverse racial and cultural strains. The American nationality seemed to him to be unquestionably English at its base—but not English as Europeans understood the word. The "well-known spleen," the stiff awkwardness and insular angularity of the English in Europe, had become modified, and by 1850 Schaff felt that "the Anglo-Saxon and Anglo-American, of all modern races, possess the strongest national character and the one best fitted for universal dominion, and that, too, not a dominion of despotism but one which makes its subjects free citizens." For the Anglo-American was both liberal and conservative, with the impulse toward freedom inseparably joined to a sense of law and order; "I doubt whether the moral influence of Christianity and of Protestantism has more deeply and widely affected any nation, than it has the Anglo-Saxon."

Considering what there was to see in America in the mid-1850s, Schaff was either deluding himself or seeing very deeply indeed. The nation which he believed on its way toward "universal dominion" seemed then to be demonstrating that it could not even maintain secure dominion over its own acres. The Kansas-Nebraska act was jarring the country toward division, and the impulse toward law and order was not strong enough to prevent the wildest sort of lawlessness and disorder along the Kansas frontier. To forecast a great world role for such a country at such a time took an uncommonly perceptive glance.

Schaff was undismayed. He could see trouble ahead, as

clearly as anyone could, but he probably would have agreed with Mr. Wiltse's finding: the die had already been cast. He believed the Americans were up to something immense: "They wrestle with the most colossal projects. The deepest meaning and aim of their political institutions are to actualize the idea of universal sovereignty, the education of every individual for intellectual and moral self-government and thus for true freedom." Confidently, he asserted that "the grandest destiny is evidently reserved for such a people." Then, as briskly as if the impending time of troubles had already been passed, he proclaimed:

> In short, if anywhere in the wide world a new page of universal history has been unfolded and a new fountain opened, fraught with incalculable curses or blessings for future generations, it is in the Republic of the United States with her starspangled banner. Either humanity has no earthly future and everything is tending to destruction, or this future lies—I say not exclusively, but mainly—in America, according to the victorious march of history, with the sun from east to west.

# Jeff Davis: The Man Behind the Image*

## June 1967

In its long gallery of memorable men, American history contains no figure quite like that of Jefferson Davis. Here is the tragic hero incarnate, the man who endured and lost a struggle more than life-size, his own defeat embodying a defeat shared by many others, until at last his unwavering endurance is about all that is remembered of him. His ordinary human qualities get flaked away, we look at stoicism and courage until it begins to seem that there is nothing else to look at, and the man takes on a marble-statue quality that is essentially bloodless. Most of the time we look in vain for the warm, passionate man who existed somewhere behind the struggle. The resulting image is admirable but it seems to be without warmth.

This is not simply because Davis, as president of the Southern Confederacy and embodiment of the Lost Cause, was by the very nature of things destined to survive as an abstraction. After all, Robert E. Lee is a tragic hero from the same epoch, and although Lee has a certain graven-image quality of his own he is nevertheless remembered with abiding affection and has a warm place in America's memory. Davis was different. He locked himself in behind a self-

* *American Heritage* magazine, June 1967

control so complete that it seemed to lock everyone else out. He could win deep devotion from others, as his relationship with Lee proves, and he could also win deep hatred, as in his relationship with General Joseph E. Johnston; yet we think of him as an iceberg, forgetting that neither love nor hate is ordinarily inspired by the frigid. Perhaps it is about time for us to take a longer look at him.

The means for doing this are at hand in an excellent and fascinating book, *Jefferson Davis: Private Letters, 1823–1889,*\* selected and edited by Hudson Strode. Culling through a vast stack of letters, most of which have never been made public before, Mr. Strode lets Davis speak for himself from his early youth to the final years of his life, and the man thus speaking and spoken for emerges as someone quite unlike the legendary person we usually see. The austere integrity and the aloof dignity are still there, but as we read these letters—most of them exchanged by Davis and his devoted wife, Varina Howell Davis—we suddenly realize that this man had both warmth and tenderness in an extraordinary degree. He had qualities, in short, that were rarely shown to outsiders, and it was simply his fate to become so completely a public man that most other people had to be and remain outsiders. His private life existed within an opaque barrier. Now the barrier comes down.

One of his problems apparently was the fact that during the eventful war years he was miscast.

As a planter and a spokesman for the Deep South, Davis had been active in politics before secession, both in the Senate and in a presidential Cabinet, but he was a West Pointer with combat experience in war and he seems, underneath everything, to have thought of himself as a soldier. In January, 1861, when he resigned from the United States Senate, he quietly dedicated himself to the service of the emerging Confederacy, but he believed that what would be

---

\* *Jefferson Davis: Private Letters, 1823–1889*, selected and edited by Hudson Strode. Harcourt, Brace & World, Inc. 580 pp.

required of him would be to lead troops in the field. He wrote to a Northern friend at this time, saying: "Civil war has only horror for me, but whatever circumstances demand shall be met as a duty and I trust be so discharged that you will not be ashamed of our former connection or cease to be my friend."

Shortly after this he was notified that he had been made president of the new Confederate government. The news came to him when he and Mrs. Davis were in the rose garden of Davis' Mississippi plantation, and Mrs. Davis said that as he read the telegram he took on an expression that made her feel that some dreadful calamity had taken place, and when he told her what the telegram said he spoke "as a man might speak of a sentence of death." His concept of duty compelled him to accept, but this was not the role he had wanted, and years after the war he wrote of the presidency that "notwithstanding my years of political service I had no fondness for it, and felt always a distaste for its belongings."

What sort of general Davis would have made, if his fate had given him that part, is of course beyond telling, although considering everything it seems likely that he might have done very well. But he was obviously not ideally fitted to be the chief political leader of a brand new country which contained as many divisive factions and clamorous personalities as the Confederate government did. To fight and win an all-out war, this government dedicated to an extreme states' rights position had to become centralized, with almost dictatorial powers vested in the executive. To accomplish this without estranging some of the most vocal and determined leaders of the South called for a suppleness, a political agility, and a flair for compromise that Davis never pretended to possess.

His years in American politics had always been rather special. He had never had the rough-and-tumble experience of workaday politics at the courthouse and statehouse level

—the kind of experience that was such an enormous asset to his opposite number, Abraham Lincoln—and as the war grew harder and put a constantly increasing strain on the fabric of the Confederacy this lack was a profound handicap. His relations with the Confederate congress became progressively worse. His everlasting efforts to muster manpower and industrial resources to oppose the overpowering Federal forces met increasing opposition from men who believed that the only hope was to give up things like the military draft and rely entirely on the old volunteer spirit and on purely inspirational leadership. In the end, the political house collapsed just as the military house collapsed, and when full night came down, a large and outspoken section of the Southern leadership considered that the defeat was mostly Davis' fault.

Richmond had to be given up, at last, the dream of an independent nation had to be given up with it, and Davis was a fugitive looking vainly for a place where a dispossessed Confederate president could dig in his heels and make a stand. There was no such place. Lee had surrendered, and so had Johnston, and Davis finally saw that his chief care now was not for a defeated cause but for his wife and children. To Varina, as he moved hopelessly across the Carolinas late in April of 1865, he wrote as follows:

> . . . I have prayed to our Heavenly Father to give me wisdom and fortitude equal to the demands of the position in which Providence has placed me. I have sacrificed so much for the cause of the Confederacy that I can measure my ability to make any further sacrifice required, and am assured there is but one to which I am not equal—my wife and children. How are they to be saved from degradation of want is now my care.

Varina bore up under all of this with a stout heart, and as the final shadows were falling she made light of her own predicament: "It is surely not the fate to which you invited me in brighter days, but you must remember that you did not invite me to a great Hero's home, but to that of a plain farmer. I have shared all your triumphs, been the *only* beneficiary of them, now I am but claiming the privilege for the first time of being all to you now these pleasures have passed for me."

It did no good. Davis was captured in southern Georgia and was taken up to Fort Monroe for imprisonment. Here his captors began to overplay their hand. They accused Davis of having had a hand in Lincoln's assassination, for a time they put leg irons on him, they kept guards and bright lights in his cell—and slowly, bit by bit, Southerners who had felt that Davis was responsible for their defeat began to see him as a martyr. It came very slowly, and after a year in prison Davis sent Varina this anguished letter: "Next to the consciousness of rectitude, it is to me the greatest of earthly consolations to know that those for whom I acted and suffer, approved and sympathize. It is common in cases of public calamity, for those who feel the infliction, to seek for some object on which to throw the blame, and rarely has it happened that the selection has been justly or generously made."

In the oddest way, Davis at last regained his liberty.

He had adjusted himself to the idea that he might have to die as a traitor, and he wrote: "Oftentimes the question occurs to me, would the spirit of vengeance be satiated by my sacrifice so that my family and countrymen would then be left in peace. If so, I trust my past life will bring others to the conclusion that is embodied in the mental answer I have so often made, and that those who would mourn me longest would least expect or desire me to shrink from the purchase." But by the spring of 1867, when it was obviously time either to bring the man to trial or to release him, there had been a change, and although the radical Republicans now controlled the Federal government it began to be clear that the last thing these people wanted was to convict Davis of treason.

The theory on which Lincoln had fought the war was that the Southern states had never actually left the Union. They could not leave it, because the Union was unbreakable; individuals might be in rebellion, but the states could not be and had not been. Now the radicals had a different notion: the states had done it, by doing it they had committed suicide, and so the government in Washington could treat them as conquered provinces and could impose on them any sort of rule it saw fit to impose. But if, in the middle of all this, the government hanged an individual for treason, it would be going back to the earlier theory, and the states as states would be relieved of guilt. Accordingly, in the middle of May, 1867, Davis was freed.

He joined Varina in Canada, went thence to England—and began to look about for a job. What does the president of a non-existent nation do for a living, when he has a wife and children to support? For a full decade this was a problem. For a time Davis served as president of an insurance company in Tennessee. He was a fish out of water, and he confessed to Varina that there was a great difference "between a man of business and a Soldier, or a Planter, or a Senator, or a Cabinet Minister, or a President, or even an exiled representative of an oppressed people." It came hard, because this man's pride was strong, and he wrote frankly: "I have compounded with my pride for the material interest of my family, and am ready to go on to the end as may best promote their happiness."

Unfortunately, the end of this venture was not far off. The Panic of 1873 put the insurance company in deep trouble. Davis resigned, returned to London, thought for a time that he had a connection as American representative of a British business firm but found that the British businessmen at last grew frightened because of "a secret dread of displeasing the Yankees." He came back to the United States, dabbled for a time in a company preparing to exploit mineral deposits in Arkansas, spent several years in the fruitless attempt to organize a Mississippi Valley association designed to promote direct trade between the valley states and England, saw it fail at last because that same "secret dread" afflicted British capitalists . . . and finally, late in the 1870s, settled down at Beauvoir in Mississippi, on the Gulf coast, to write his memoirs.

This book, a two-volume affair called *The Rise and Fall of the Confederate Government,* came out in 1881. It did not make a fortune for him—the North, where American books were mostly reviewed and bought, was not yet ready to admit that the one-time Confederate president had anything to say that anybody needed to listen to—but Davis found himself able to support his family, and in his final years he got a measure of peace and happiness. The climax came in 1886 and 1887, when Davis appeared in public at the dedication of Confederate monuments in Montgomery, Atlanta, Savannah, and Macon. Suddenly, and apparently quite unexpectedly, he found himself the hero of the South. He was no longer the president who had failed to win the war: he was the man who had kept the faith, who had endured years of imprisonment, who had behaved with dignity and integrity during the time that followed, who in his book had stood firmly by the cause he had led—and, all in all, he was again the man he had been at Montgomery in 1861, when crowds stood to cheer the very sight of him.

Davis died in 1889. On the day of his death his daughter Winnie, in Paris, knowing that he was ill but not realizing that he was so near the end, sent him a letter closing with these words:

> . . . when I am away from you I can only think, and think, and love you for your goodness and tenderness, with which you covered me as with a cloak all through

my childhood, screening my faults and answering my unreasonable questions with always an honest reply, the rarest thing given to a child in the world. And so I will end by saying, as I began, "My darling father." Good night.

Need it be repeated? There was a warm and tender human being behind the reserved individual who set so much store by "the consciousness of rectitude."

# III

# Our American Heritage*

## 1964

*On July 26, 1964, an official state historical marker, dealing with Benzonia's now-vanished institution of higher education which was successively known as Grand Traverse College, Benzonia College, and Benzonia Academy, was dedicated. The marker, which is located on what was once the college campus and is now Benzonia's village park, adjacent to US-31, was purchased with funds provided by the Benzonia Garden Club and by alumni of the institution. The text reads:*

### BENZONIA COLLEGE

In 1858, in what was then a remote wilderness, the Rev. Charles E. Bailey and four families from his Ohio Congregational parish founded Benzonia colony. It was to be an "educational Christian colony" modeled after the earlier Congregational settlements at Oberlin, Ohio, and Olivet, Michigan. As an integral part of the new community, Grand Traverse College was chartered in 1863. Its first building was erected on this corner. During the pioneer era it provided college preparatory work and teacher training. The school reorganized as Ben-

* *Michigan History*, XLVII Michigan Historical Commission, December 1964

zonia College in 1891. It supplied college-level education until 1900. Benzonia Academy was then maintained
until changed conditions led to its closing in 1918. Benzonia College and Academy fulfilled the founders'
dream of bringing educational opportunity to northern
Michigan.

Michigan Historical Commission Registered Site No. 245

*Although it is nearly half a century since Benzonia
Academy closed its doors, a surprising number of graduates of the school turned out for the occasion. Among
them was the academy's best-known alumnus, the Pulit-
zer Prize-winning Civil War historian and senior editor
of* American Heritage *magazine, Bruce Catton. A native
of Petoskey, where he was born on October 9, 1899, Mr.
Catton graduated from Benzonia Academy with the class
of 1916. His attachment to the institution is closer than
that of most graduates, however, since his father,
George R. Catton, was the last head of Benzonia Academy. Mr. Catton's older brother, the Rev. William Robert Catton, also an academy alumnus and chairman of
the dedication program, cautioned all participants ahead
of time to confine themselves to a "few well chosen
words." Those of Bruce Catton follow. [Editor.]*

I do not think we need an extended speech here today.
The men whose achievements we are commemorating were
accustomed to speak for themselves, and they spoke with a
good deal of eloquence, both in words and in deeds. We
ourselves are here today because of that eloquence. Something this summer called to us, out of the past, and we
had to listen to it because it once helped to shape our lives.
The little institution which struggled so bravely on this
hilltop went out of existence nearly half a century ago, but
the best part of it lives on in our hearts.

So we are not simply paying a sentimental tribute to

something that is gone forever. We are testifying to something important in our own origins; the little story of this college and academy is a small but significant part of the larger American story. It means more than it seems to mean.

The men who came here more than a century ago to found this institution lighted a small fire as a beacon on the edge of a great wilderness. They were part of the dedicated army of Americans who wage war on darkness, who spend themselves in pushing the shadows back so that the people who come after them will not always have to walk in the twilight. We ourselves have had firsthand experience of the value of the light which that beacon shed. We could see our own paths through life a bit more clearly because of what was given us here; if we live up to what was given us, we in our turn may pass a little of that light on for still another generation.

In any case, we need to see this Benzonia story as a typical part of the great American process. People are always doing what these founders did and the land is dotted with their handiwork. Sometimes they meet with great success, and sometimes they are what their critical descendants call failures; that is, sometimes the institutions they found grow great and live on and on, and sometimes it is all over in a generation or two and nothing remains but a little marker by the roadside—a marker, and certain memories in the hearts of people like ourselves who are not far from going on to join the great majority.

And yet "failure" is not at all the word to use for any of these ventures. Add them all together and you get one of the undying sources of our national strength—one of the things that even in our gloomiest times enables us to look to the future with hope.

For the wilderness against which these beacons are lighted —the wilderness that encompassed this little college in the hour of its birth—was not just the physical, visible wilderness of pines and hardwoods which then covered most of this state. That wilderness was something that could be dealt with by the lumbermen, the landlookers and the land buyers, the men with double-bitted axes and crosscut saws. They did deal with it; the wilderness is gone forever, and nobody needed to start any kind of educational institution to help in its destruction.

The wilderness this college and academy were concerned with was something less tangible and also much more dangerous: the darkness that exists in the minds of human beings, the ignorance that cripples and enslaves men, the simple and tragic lack of knowledge that can keep men from realizing their true potential; the deep midnight that can possess the human heart when faith and inspiration have never been provided.

There was no ambitious attempt here to create a great and enduring center of learning; this was just an effort to enable the people of an isolated society to walk by a better light, and we should never forget that the light sometimes was needed very badly indeed. Life on the frontier—and this region was a true frontier, even in the time of our own childhoods—was no happy golden age. I remember as a boy overhearing a conversation between my father and Professor William J. Hutchins of Oberlin College. They had been talking about the crippling limitations that beset people who lived in the cheerless villages created by the lumber boom, and Professor Hutchins remarked that while it was commonly said that God made the country and man made the city, it ought to be added that sometimes the Devil himself made the small town; to which my father readily agreed, saying that he had seen some prime examples of the Devil's own handiwork.

That remark would not have much point today. The old isolation is gone, the physical wilderness has vanished and its debris has been cleared up—and the old darkness of mind and heart has been diminished, too, because of the work done by just such tiny and valiant enterprises as the one that lived on this hilltop.

No, we do not use the word "failure." What was done here was done well. It succeeded perhaps better than any of the men who had a part in it could know, and its influence goes on and on. The little fire that was lighted here did indeed go out, at last—but behold! the land is brighter, and it always will be. One part of the darkness is gone forever.

And that is the way it goes, with things like this. Over and over, all across America, men fight to push the shadows back. The men themselves die, the physical traces of their presence disappear—but the place where they worked is lighter because of what they did. They leave light behind them; and some day, because of it, we believe that there will be, in the hearts of men, light enough to build the beautiful city of God.

# A World of Wonder*

## April 1959

Deeply embedded in the history of America there is a
strange quality of expectancy. We have somehow inherited
a sense of wonder, a feeling that our strange progress toward
the future is a fantastic and incomprehensible adventure that
moves constantly past the bounds of imagination. We are
permanently oriented, so to speak, in the direction of the
improbable, and the fact that we do not always know what
to do when the improbable turns out to be real makes very
little difference. From the moment of our beginning we
have been looking for something on the far side of the
horizon—from which it follows that we are never convinced
that any horizon is ever final.

This is in large part our heritage from the open sea.
America could not exist until somebody went questing
for it. It had to be discovered, and the discovery required
an undying curiosity and a prodigious act of faith. Someone,
in other words, had to get in a ship and go out beyond the
limits of knowledge. When he had gone as far as he could
go, other men had to do likewise; and for the better part
of five centuries the American story has been bright with
the names of great voyages.

* *American Heritage* magazine, April 1959

Greatest of all, of course, was the first one, the earth-changing voyage of Christopher Columbus in 1492. The story is almost too familiar to us. It is one of the first stories drummed into us in school. The great Admiral and his three little ships, *Santa Maria, Pinta,* and *Niña,* move out from Palos like shapes in a pageant, romantic but vaguely unreal. We learn how Queen Isabella pawned certain jewels to make the voyage possible, how the sailors feared the unknown and came close to mutiny, how the Admiral saw a light on the dark sky line just when hope seemed lost, and how at last this man who had found an authentic new world believed that he had simply reached the East Indies—conceiving, as do most of us, that the world holds fewer surprises than is really the case. We get, in short, the familiar legend, and we let it go at that; which is a pity, for here is one of the most significant stories in all American history, the story that sets the key for everything that has happened since.

It is a good story to return to, and an excellent approach is to be found in the biography which Columbus' son Ferdinand wrote in the 1530s, some years after the Admiral's death. Translated and annotated by Benjamin Keen, *The Life of the Admiral Christopher Columbus*\* is now available to the general reader.

Why did Columbus go on that immense voyage in the first place? Ferdinand explains succinctly: "Turning to the reasons which persuaded the Admiral to undertake the discovery of the Indies, I say there were three, namely, natural reasons, the authority of writers, and the testimony of sailors." The natural reasons were simple enough; Columbus knew that the earth was a globe and believed that a good sailor could circumnavigate it. The "authority of writers" was a shakier foundation; he relied on things set down by Aristotle, Seneca, Strabo, Marco Polo, and others, and not

---

\* *The Life of the Admiral Christopher Columbus,* by his son Ferdinand, translated and annotated by Benjamin Keen. Rutgers University Press. 316 pp.

all of these knew what they were talking about. One sus-
pects that it was the testimony of sailors that really got
him. Atlantic seaports were full of fables and tall tales
about men who had ventured to the west, a hodgepodge
of yarns about lost islands, floating bits of carved wood,
inexplicable landfalls made by storm-tossed mariners, including a fine yarn told by a one-eyed sailor who believed
that on a voyage to Ireland he had touched the coast of
Tatary. There were hints, in plenty, that something besides
the great gulf lay west of the Atlantic sky line, and Columbus wanted to find out.

Well, Columbus got his way, and at last he and his
three ships went cruising; and when they made their landfall the sense of wonder re-entered the world, so that human
life took on a permanent new dimension. . . .

> At daybreak they saw an island about fifteen leagues in
> length, very level, full of green trees and abounding in
> springs, with a large lake in the middle, and inhabited
> by a multitude of people who hastened to the shore, as-
> tounded and marveling at the sight of the ships . . . and
> the Admiral, perceiving they were a gentle, peaceful and
> very simple people, gave them little red caps and glass
> beads which they hung about their necks, together with
> trifles that they cherished as if they were precious stones
> of great price.

The natives, Ferdinand explains, knew perfectly well that
these trinkets had no great intrinsic value. They prized
them simply because these strange newcomers had given
them to them, "for they were convinced our men had come
from Heaven, and therefore they wished to have some relic
of them."

They would be disillusioned a little later, for the Spaniards—like all other Europeans who came after them—ruled
their new possessions with a heavy hand, giving the native

residents nothing much better than a choice between slavery, dispossession, or outright extermination. Columbus seems to have lacked a social conscience; as a man of his time, he believed that the Indians must be made to serve their conquerors for their own good. Not until Las Casas would a strong voice be raised in defense of the rights of America's original inhabitants.

But if the natives were to be disillusioned, so too was Columbus himself. As voyage succeeded voyage, it began to be clear to the Spanish authorities that they had given the Admiral altogether too much, and he was whittled down. Between the first great stroke of discovery and the long, wearisome fight to maintain his own authority and prerogatives against mutinous subordinates and schemers at court, Columbus fell on difficult times. Yet the faith that was the obverse side of the coin, with him—the faith that went hand in hand with his God-given curiosity and eagerness—never deserted him. Seven years after the discovery, deserted by fortune, Columbus wrote thus in his journal:

> The day after Christmas Day, 1499, all having left me, I was attacked by the Indians and the bad Christians, and was placed in such extremity that fleeing death I took to sea in a small caravel. Then Our Lord aided me, saying, "Man of little faith, do not fear, I am with thee." And he dispersed my enemies, and showed me how I might fulfill my vows. Unhappy sinner that I am, to have placed all my hopes in the things of this world!

Actually, Columbus had placed his hopes not so much in the things of this world as in the belief that this world contained ever so much more than any of his contemporaries suspected. These hopes were abundantly sustained. The belief that went with them has colored the American consciousness ever since.

## Mariner's Quest

Between Columbus sailing west to see what might lie beyond an unknown sea, and a late nineteenth-century sea captain who, lacking gainful employment, went cruising aimlessly and alone all around a world whose last shores had been mapped and claimed, there is an immense gap. Yet it is by no means absurd to mention Joshua Slocum on the same page with Columbus, because all true voyages of discovery are basically alike. The voyager is concerned first of all with something in himself, if it is nothing more than the conviction that if he searches long enough he can make the world give him something he has not yet had.

Joshua Slocum was a Bluenose, which is to say that he was a native of Nova Scotia, a cold, hard man from the Bay of Fundy, who went to sea young, became a skipper of Yankee merchant ships, and in the 1890s discovered that the world had moved out from under him. He knew precisely how to move a wind-driven ship through all the chances of tide and water. His only trouble was that the era in which men could be paid for doing that sort of thing had ended, the era of the deep-water sailing man was over, and here was a master of his craft surviving into a day when the craft itself was one with Nineveh and Tyre.

He was, in other words, a master mariner in sail at a time when nobody had any work for master mariners in sail. So he found a tubby little 37-foot sailboat which was rotting on the beach, spent the better part of a year rebuilding it, and then got aboard, took on such provisions as he could get, and then took off on a trip around the world, singlehanded, sailing off for the last horizon at a time when nobody in particular cared whether master mariners still survived. He went from New England over to Gibraltar, cut down across the South Atlantic to the Strait

of Magellan, swung out across the Pacific to the fabulous
islands under the sun, went on to Australia and thence to
South Africa, and came plugging back four years later, a
singlehanded circumnavigator of the globe who had done
something fabulous but useless. And he wrote a book to
tell what had happened to him.

The full story of his adventures is set forth in *The Voyages
of Joshua Slocum,** by Walter Magnes Teller; a book which
not only gives Slocum's own background but reprints everything that he wrote about his experiences, and which somehow takes on stature simply because what the man did
and what was in his mind when he did it tie in with the
basic American adventure.

For Slocum resembled both Columbus and, in an odd
way, Henry David Thoreau, who roamed to the farthest
ends of the universe without actually leaving his own Massachusetts. He was devoted to solitude, which has been an
American trait from the earliest days—consider Daniel
Boone, and Richard Henry Dana, or if you choose, Abraham
Lincoln—and he found in solitude what he had been looking for: a trace of the ultimate answer, a testing of himself, a
mocking answer to the riddle posed by Aladdin's lamp:
"My fisherman's lantern, which I got at Gloucester, has
shown me better things than your smoky old burner ever
revealed." He sailed all around the world in an unsea-
worthy little tub which, a few years later, was the death
of him, and he had fun at it.

It appears that he was a man who could make friends.
Singlehanded, in a frowsty tub of a sloop, he puts in at
Gibraltar—and, suddenly, a British admiral, no man to be
impressed by a beachcombing sailor, makes him his guest,
orders the resources of the Royal Navy put at his disposal,
and sees to it that his fragile sloop is prepared for its
enormous adventure. It is the same in Buenos Aires, in

* *The Voyages of Joshua Slocum,* collected and introduced by Walter
Magnes Teller. Rutgers University Press. 401 pp.

Punta Arenas, in the islands under the sun, in Australia and in Cape Town; he comes in out of the ocean and suddenly he knows everyone and everyone is glad to help him, and he goes around the globe alone, all but penniless, and lacking resources, but somehow everybody helps him and he comes home famous, a world figure, a master mariner to whom everyone will give a helping hand.

Why? Partly, as was said, because he had the knack of making people like him; but more, it would seem, because the quest he was on was something that touched everyone, something that still has its appeal, because he was not just performing a stunt—he was looking for something which the world thought it had lost, and because he looked for it so bravely and with such simplicity of mind the world discovered that it was still there, and he got it. His awkward sloop, the *Spray*, became one with the *Golden Hind;* and at the end, after four years of lonely wandering, he got back to New England, dropped anchor in his home port of Fairhaven, Massachusetts, and wrote a paragraph about what it might have meant:

> If the *Spray* discovered no continents on her voyage, it may be that there were no more continents to be discovered; she did not seek new worlds, or sail to pow-wow about the dangers of the seas. The sea has been much maligned. To find one's way to lands already discovered is a good thing, and the *Spray* made the discovery that even the worst sea is not so terrible to a well-appointed ship. No king, no country, no treasury at all, was taxed for the voyage of the *Spray*, and she accomplished all that she undertook to do.

Which was, specifically, what? To fulfill, probably, what her captain wanted; which is to say that the true voyage of discovery depends not so much on the new landfall that may be made, or on the perils met and surpassed along the way, as on what the captain himself has in his heart when the voyage begins. Slocum had what Columbus had left for him: nothing much in the way of physical discovery, but a complete, untouched universe that could be found only in the examination of loneliness and solitude, a gateway opening into the infinite, which is finally the meaning of America.

Slocum was restless after he got home. He exhibited his vessel, posed for a time as a celebrity, picked up a few odd dollars here and there, and at last took off once more on a voyage across the trackless ocean. He never came back. In the fall of 1909, at 65, he sailed for South America, with some vague plan for wandering up the Orinoco and down the Amazon, and he never made port. The *Spray*'s ancient seams apparently opened up in some heavy sea and that was the end. Or, possibly, it was the beginning.

## Voyage To Nowhere

To complete the story, one more famous ship, and a famous voyage: the U.S.S. *Indianapolis*, an eight-inch-gun cruiser of the vintage of the early 1930s, which sailed from San Francisco in the summer of 1945, carrying a cargo which made her one of the ships that change history, and then went on to a resting place two miles under the surface of the Pacific, a tragic ship whose end was mystery and a dark portent.

The *Indianapolis* was a ship which crossed the border between yesterday and tomorrow. She died because of a thousand-to-one chance that went wrong, and her end was dark tragedy for hundreds of American families, and a plaguy problem for the United States Navy. The tragedy went unalleviated, and the problem, Heaven knows, went completely unsolved; but the ship itself went on to become one of the great, portentous vessels in the American story.

In *Abandon Ship!* * Richard F. Newcomb, an excellent war correspondent for the Associated Press, tells her story in first-rate style.

Until the summer of 1945, the *Indianapolis* was just one of many cruisers built and maintained by the U. S. Navy. Then she got a job to do: amid all of the trappings of top secrecy, she was pulled up to a pier in San Francisco and given a top-secret cargo to carry out to Guam—namely, the bits and pieces which would presently be put together to make the world's first atomic bomb, which was dropped on Hiroshima to end one era in human history and to open, cloudily but effectively, another. This, quite unintentionally, the *Indianapolis* did; then, her mission accomplished— and what warship ever had a more far-reaching mission?— the *Indianapolis* went on, with a routine assignment to go to the Philippines, indulge in a little special training, and then become one of the fleet that was going to make the final assault on the shores of Japan.

The final assault never took place, because the bits and pieces that this cruiser ferried out to Guam changed the face of the world forever, and made it unnecessary for any sea-borne fleet to blast a way in through the perimeter defenses of Japan; but it would not have mattered much in any case, because the *Indianapolis* never even reached the Philippines. A few minutes after midnight on July 30, 1945, the cruiser was steaming along in mid-Pacific; a roving Japanese submarine just happened to surface a mile away, a fitful moon just happened to break through the clouds at that precise moment, the submarine's skipper loosed two torpedoes, and the *Indianapolis* went down inside of twelve minutes, with a loss of some 800 American lives.

The loss became a *cause célèbre*, which is a high-toned way of saying that it raised an unearthly stink—partly because, as a meaningless tragedy, it was announced to the

---

* *Abandon Ship! Death of the U.S.S. Indianapolis,* by Richard F. Newcomb. Henry Holt & Co. 305 pp.

world on the very day the war ended, and partly because it quickly became painfully clear that this warship had somehow fallen through a hitherto undetected gap in the American Navy's system for handling its combat vessels in time of war. The Navy, to be blunt about it, simply lost track of this ship, for the 48 hours that really counted; because it had lost track of it, a good many members of the crew who might otherwise have been saved lost their lives; and the United States Navy, which could admit anything on earth except a flaw in its basic system for handling combat ships, made itself look infernally bad hunting for a few scapegoats who could be compelled to take the blame for the disaster.

Seldom has the Navy looked worse than it looked when it tried to explain this disaster away. It court-martialed the cruiser's captain, broke him, and then, half-apologetically, took it all back—the poor man's career was wrecked, but if it helped he had the consolation of knowing that the Navy didn't really mean it. Then it pounced on four underlings, blasted them, and finally had to backtrack on that action. What it could not do—what no military organization can ever do—was admit that it had simply muffed one, not because of any individual failure but because the system which it had set up for moving ships from here to there in time of war had one unsuspected hole in it.

With all of this Mr. Newcomb deals at length, thoroughly and, I think, conclusively. Yet what sticks with one, when the tragic story is finished, is the realization that here, in the long history of American seafaring, was one of history's fated ships: a ship which served as a hinge on which human history turned, and which, its mission accomplished, went to the bottom of the sea, with all its freight of human grief and suffering.

For the *Indianapolis*, like the *Santa Maria*, was sailing toward the wholly improbable. Before this cruiser left San Francisco, life was lived on one set of terms; after it went to the bottom, the terms on which people live had been transvalued, and nothing will ever be the same again. Nobody in this ship's crew knew it, and if any had known it most of them would not have had much time to meditate about it, but the voyage of the *Indianapolis* was a cutoff point. Before that, one kind of life: after that, another kind.

We live today in a time when this new kind of life is giving us nightmares. Yet if any people on earth should be prepared to enter into change of this kind, it is the Americans. Once more, a horizon has been fractured; once more, the attainable bounds of human experience have been pushed back infinitely far. We were born that way. If now we face a time of danger and challenge, it may also be a time of enormous opportunity. Here we are, after five centuries, face to face with a world of wonder.

# The Men Who Made Canoes*

## February 1965

The interests that impel a man to dig into the shadowed corners of the past can be obscure, and what he finds there may not always seem worth the effort. Yet light can come from unlikely places, especially when it falls on a primitive society that kept no records and never bothered to try to explain itself. Simply to know how stone-age people made the things they used can put those people in a new perspective. Suddenly in place of an untutored savage we can see a man, with emotions and intelligence like our own, painfully doing his best to cope with a hostile world. Seeing him so, we see our kinship with him, and history's mysterious continuity begins to mean more.

Thus: In 1887 a young Ohioan named Edwin Tappan Adney went to the New Brunswick woods on vacation and discovered that what he wanted more than anything else was to learn all that could be learned about that most characteristic of all Indian artifacts, the birch-bark canoe. How did the Indians devise this craft? How did they make it, back in the days before the white man's ideas and techniques ever reached them? How did they get and transmit

* *American Heritage* magazine, February 1965

their skills? What, in short, has the birch-bark canoe to tell us about the people who invented and perfected it?

Adney spent most of his remaining sixty years finding out. He moved to Canada and became a Canadian citizen, learned to speak a number of Indian tongues, visited canoe-making peoples all across the north country, made sketches and notes, built canoes himself the way the Indians did, and became probably the greatest authority on this subject that ever lived. He never completed his studies, but he left a huge mass of papers, models, and sketches, and fortunately all of this material was finally deposited with the Mariners Museum at Newport News, Virginia. The museum authorities then did the best thing imaginable and called in Howard I. Chapelle, curator of transportation at the Smithsonian, and Chapelle put together a book, using Adney's fabulous research material and his own vast knowledge of ship design. The result: *The Bark Canoes and Skin Boats of North America,* which sounds as if it might be dry as dust but which instead is wholly fascinating.

To begin with, the birch-bark canoe itself was fabulous. It was light, fast, fragile but easily repaired, as odorous of the north woods as a bed made of balsam boughs; it could float in the shallowest water but it could carry a heavy load, it could be picked up and carried from one waterway to another without wearing anybody out, it served both the lone hunter and the prowling war party, it managed to be delicate and tough at the same time, and it passed into romance before Americans even began to suspect that the north country was romantic.

It was also an extremely sophisticated creation. The red man who invented and used it was no fumbling troglodyte. He knew precisely what he was about and he devised a unique way to make boats, perfectly adapted to the materials he had to use.

* *The Bark Canoes and Skin Boats of North America,* by Edwin Tappan Adney and Howard I. Chapelle. The Smithsonian Institution. 242 pp. Illustrated.

Except for the log dugout (and its modern analogue, the one-piece craft cast in plastic), virtually every other boat ever built was constructed around a rigid framework. First there had to be a keel, with stem and stern pieces, and then there would be ribs, held firmly together with longitudinal stringers, knees, beams, and all the rest—a literal skeleton, taking shape piece by piece, with the outer covering going on last of all. Take away the covering—the skin, the carefully fitted planking, or what not—and the skeleton remained, ready to be given a new covering if that was desired. From rowboat on up to Atlantic liner, the skeleton was what mattered.

The Indian simply did not do it that way. He never made a keel, and what skeleton the canoe had came last. Essentially the canoe was an envelope of birch bark stitched to the gunwales, with ribs and sheathing added simply to keep the bark taut and to prevent the occupant from accidentally putting his foot or his bottom through the outer skin. The skeleton was held in place by the bark; strip the bark off a canoe and everything but the gunwales would fly apart.

It would seem to be impossible to make a satisfactory boat that way, but the Indian succeeded, creating something that was graceful, beautiful, and completely suited to its uses. The canoe was not in the least like the early Briton's coracle or the buffalo-hide bullboat of the western plains— a clumsy butter dish whose occupant was just one degree better off than he would have been if he had straddled a log and paddled with his hands. The canoe was a craft whose design no naval architect has ever been able to improve materially, and when the first white men got to America they took to it with enthusiasm, and they used it without change for centuries. Today's canoe is made of materials the Indian never heard of, but its basic pattern has not been altered very much. The Indian could neither draw a plan nor write specifications, but he needed no lessons from anybody.

He took his materials where he found them, which limited the area in which the authentic canoe was used: if
the right trees were not handy, there could be no canoes.
The essential, of course, was birch bark: the bark, that is,
of the white or paper birch, the beautiful tree that gets into
all of the summer resort photographs and sketches. With
this, the Indian had to have white cedar for the ribs, sheathing, and usually for the gunwales; maple for the thwarts;
roots of black spruce, white cedar, tamarack, or jack pine
for stitchings and lashings; and spruce gum melted down
with animal fat to make the seams watertight. Some tribes
not blessed with many birches made do with other barks,
but nothing but birch bark was really satisfactory, and they
usually got their canoes by trading with more northern
tribes; otherwise, they used dugouts.

The Indian had to work hard to make a canoe, because
the tools he used were abominable. For an axe he had nothing but a blade of chipped stone lashed to a wooden handle;
he used stone knives, wedges of stone or wood, and wooden
mauls to drive them; awls and drills he made from bone or
whatever else was handy. Sometimes he used the paired
incisor teeth of the beaver for a chisel, with the skull for a
handle—the beaver having previously, of course, been dispossessed. To cut down a tree—and a birch big enough to
provide usable sheets of bark could be pretty big—and
then to remove the bark and to split out, dress, and smooth
the timbers for gunwales, ribs, thwarts, and interior sheathing, must have been unutterably wearisome.

If he had a large birch and proposed to make a small
canoe, the Indian could sometimes get one sheet of bark
big enough to serve his purposes. Otherwise he had to get a
number of separate sheets; and in either case he usually
soaked the bark in water until he was ready to use it, in
order to keep it pliable. (He also soaked the snaky roots
that would be used for stitching and lashing, for the same
reason.) It was best, by the way, to get the bark after a

long winter thaw, or early in the spring when the sap had begun to flow, because it had more elasticity then.

Once he had his materials in hand, the builder got to work. His building yard was a smooth bit of ground near the water, preferably shaded so that the hot sun would not dry out the bark too fast, and near a good camping site because the Indian was going to be there for many days and had to have a convenient place to sleep and eat. Usually he made his gunwales first, splitting out the long pieces of wood, tapering them and rounding the edges, usually laminating them in the middle for greater strength, lashing the ends together, and springing the gunwales apart for the required breadth by making the thwarts and mortising them in place.

All of this done, the Indian laid his joined gunwales on the building bed and drove strong stakes into the ground all around, from end to end, accurately outlining the boat's final shape. Stakes and gunwales were then removed, the bark was laid on the bed, and the gunwales were laid on top of it, weighted down with stones, to serve temporarily as a frame that would give the birch-bark envelope its proper shape. The edges of the bark were slashed here and there and the bark was bent upward, at which point the stakes were put back into their original holes. Then gores were cut in the bark, any additional strips or panels of bark that might be needed were added, and the bark was carefully stitched together. Then the gunwales were taken out, sheered up at the proper height, and the upper edge of the envelope was stitched and lashed to the gunwales, and the stakes were removed.

Now the result began to look like a canoe, except that it was flat-bottomed and wall-sided, with angles where there ought to be curves. The seams were gummed on the inside, stem and stern pieces were fitted, and long strips of thin, white cedar sheathing were laid along the bottom and sides, held in place by temporary ribs while the permanent ribs were prepared. There might be fifty permanent ribs, thin, wide cedar battens that were treated with boiling water until they became malleable and then were bent into shape and allowed to dry. The temporary ribs were removed and the permanent ones were inserted, mortised into the gunwales, and given a snug force-fit, pinning the sheathing into shape and giving the hull its final form, with rounding bilges and a smooth, moderate curvature across the bottom.

While this was being done the Indian had to keep the bark and stitching wet so that the skin would bend and not crack under the strain; he also had to know just how much strain the bark would take without bursting, and he had to know—by sighting along the hull or by running his hands over it—when the curves were right, when the craft was symmetrical, when, in short, the thing was properly shipshape, with no uncalled-for bulges in the hull and with a graceful sheer line. After he was satisfied, he fastened thin strips of cedar on top of the gunwales for added strength and neatness, turned the canoe upside down, and gummed the seams on the outside to make them fully watertight—and then, once he had made some paddles, the canoe was ready for use.

The design followed partly the builder's own preference, partly the use to which the canoe was to be put. On open water, low ends were good, to avoid wind resistance; to run the rapids, high ends would keep waves from breaking in over the bow. If there was to be a good deal of portaging, high ends were useful: at night, the canoe turned bottom-up would lie far enough off the ground to provide the bearer with shelter. A canoe built for salt water might have a hogged sheer—that is, its sides would be higher amidships than at the ends, so that the occupant could draw a heavy weight in over the sides, a net full of fish or a harpooned seal, without being swamped by a rush of water over low gunwales. Tribal fashions varied, too. Some Indians liked canoes with a sharp V-bottom and flaring topsides, and others preferred a bottom almost flat with a good deal of tumble home above the bilges. But all of them knew exactly what they were doing.

Proof of this can be seen in the way the French put the canoe to work. The famous fur trade, carried on for two centuries or more, could not have existed without the birch-bark canoe. The French gave the Indian modern tools and put him to work, and he turned out cargo-carrying craft thirty-six feet long and capable of bearing from two to three tons of freight besides the crew, but light enough to be portaged by four men. Using these, the fur companies opened the north country, virtually exterminated the beaver, turned tribal cultures inside out, and during generation after generation carried on one of the most picturesque and romantic trades the North American continent ever saw.

It was romantic from a distance; at close range it was a man-killer. The men who paddled these canoes were overworked, badly fed, and pitilessly exploited. At the portages, which were numerous, a good man was supposed to lug at least 180 pounds of freight (twice that much, very often) up hill and down dale, and the packer's working life was very short. The fur brigades put a splash of color on the landscape from Montreal to Saskatchewan, but the individual members of these brigades paid a high price for it.

Originally the Indian did little to decorate his canoe, except that he might make a little design representing his personal mark, or signature, somewhere near the bow or stern by scraping away the outer layer of bark according to a set pattern. Some tribes liked to use porcupine-quill designs here and there, and some ran decorations along the sides just below the gunwales. A war canoe, usually carrying four warriors off on a raid, might have each man's personal mark somewhere on its sides; if it carried a chief, only the chief's mark would be applied.

Nothing else that the Indian made called for as much work and care as the birch-bark canoe, and in consequence it was something he valued highly. A touching illustration of this fact is provided by a discovery made about a century ago on the east coast of Newfoundland, when an Indian burial cave was found. In this cave a small boy had been buried, and his parents did their best to send their love off with him when he departed. In the cave, beside his body, there was a wooden image of the boy, toy bows and arrows, little packages of food—and a model canoe, three feet long, as carefully made as any canoe might be. Thus equipped, the youngster was left to make his last journey.

# The Swordbearers*

## April 1965

Undertaking to examine "the decisive effect of individual human character on history," the British writer Corelli Barnett reaches a glum conclusion. In his excellent book, *The Swordbearers,*† he studies four famous leaders of the First World War—Colonel-General Helmuth von Moltke, Admiral Sir John Jellicoe, General Philippe Pétain, and General Erich Ludendorff—and his moral seems to be that these men were thrown into crises that were simply too big for them. Their impact on history came largely because of their own inability to measure up to an overwhelming challenge.

It was not altogether their fault. They had to direct the enormous instruments of mass power which modern Europe had developed, and these instruments were all but uncontrollable. Immense technological proficiency was in the hands of a society that was politically and socially obsolescent. These men could not rise above the level of that society, and in the end they destroyed what they were trying to save. Leadership of an extraordinary kind was demanded of them, and unfortunately they were just average leaders.

* *American Heritage* magazine, April 1965
† *The Swordbearers: Supreme Command in the First World War*, by Correlli Barnett. William Morrow and Company. 392 pp.

Moltke, for instance, had to execute the famous Schlieffen Plan, which was supposed to bring Germany a quick, decisive victory over France. (Whatever else World War I might have done, its effect would certainly have been infinitely different if it had ended in two months.) Moltke was probably the wrong man for the job; far from being the blood-and-iron war lord of Prussian military tradition, he was sensitive, subject to paralysis simply because he saw his innumerable problems in too great detail.

But the job itself was wrong. Once Germany's magnificently prepared armies went into France, they got beyond the reach of headquarters. Communications broke down, and presently each army was acting on its own. They were fighting a twentieth-century war under the conditions of Napoleon's day; trained to render implicit obedience to detailed orders from the high command, they got off into a confusing melee where fragmentary orders based on imperfect knowledge reached them too late to be of any use. When they moved across Germany these armies went by train, with every detail of supply and transportation elaborately arranged; when they moved across France they went on foot, services of supply collapsed, the soldiers themselves were marched out of their shoes, and in the end they lost the Battle of the Marne from a combination of utter exhaustion and the lack of coherent direction. Moltke was the victim not so much of his own inadequacies as of an impossible situation.

Pétain was another sensitive soldier, who found himself given supreme command in France in 1917 just at the moment when the French Army was beginning to mutiny. Heaven knows it had reason enough for a mutinous state of mind, and Pétain served his country ably by devoting himself simply to keeping the army in existence, saving its manpower, and waiting for the rising tide of Allied power to save the day. The trouble here was that he was confirmed in a defeatist psychology. He kept France from falling out of the war then, but a generation later, called on once again to serve in a time of catastrophe, he could be nothing more than the architect of defeat.

Ludendorff defeated himself, as Mr. Barnett sees it. An expert tactician, he mastered the secret of winning tactical successes, brought the German war machine close to victory in 1918, lost sight of his strategic goals in his obsession with purely tactical achievements, found at last that he had used up the strength that was needed to turn these achievements into final triumph, and then gave way to panic. He had none of Moltke's or Pétain's brooding sensitivity, but his toughness was brittle and it broke under strain. Once he realized that Germany's strength was ebbing and that Allied power was immeasurably increasing, and that his own powerful offensive was not going to bring a quick decision, he threw in his hand. The immediate cause of Germany's surrender in November, 1918, was not the legendary "stab in the back" inflicted by defeatist elements at home, but the abject collapse of the will of General Ludendorff.

Of the commanders whom Mr. Barnett studies here, the most interesting by all odds is Admiral Jellicoe. Not only was he a much more appealing character than these others; he seems also to have been more intelligent, and his great handicap was the fact that he realized all too well—as few other men did at the time—that the famous British Navy which was his to command was actually (in Mr. Barnett's expressive phrase) a "flawed cutlass." It simply was not as good as it was supposed to be, and that knowledge kept Jellicoe from taking advantage of the opportunity that opened to him at Jutland.

The British Navy was the victim of its own imposing tradition. For a century it had not fought, except for minor "police actions" here and there, and Mr. Barnett sums it up with cruel frankness: "The navy was no longer a deadly functional instrument of policy; it was an exclusive yacht club." It was a spit-and-polish organization, most of whose officers blandly assumed that no other navy was comparable to it, and over the years it had gone badly to seed. To be sure, Sir John Fisher came in as First Sea Lord in 1904 and gave it a merciless shaking-up, and when he left, Winston Churchill arrived and carried the process further, but the time had not been long enough. As one of Fisher's protégés, Jellicoe knew that most of the defects had not been remedied.

Many of the Navy's finest ships were poorly designed, engineering was faulty, protection was defective, ordnance development had lagged, and in the science of gunnery the new German Navy was far ahead. In matériel and in training, the Germans had better torpedoes and knew more about how to use them, and at the time the war began, Jellicoe privately confessed that "it is highly dangerous to consider that our ships as a whole are superior or even equal fighting machines."

This unhappy belief shaped everything Jellicoe did. He adopted a highly conservative course, both in strategy and in tactics; he would force no action to a conclusion, he would take no chances with German submarines or torpedo attacks, he would play it safe all the way. With his flawed cutlass he would not try to strike a blow so heavy that the cutlass might break.

At Jutland the German High Seas Fleet was at his mercy. That is, he had put the much larger British fleet between the Germans and their home base, under circumstances which offered him a dazzling victory that would have had far-reaching effects. With the High Seas Fleet removed from the water, Britain could have patrolled the North Sea so closely that the desperate German submarine war, which came a year later, could not have been tried; as Mr. Barnett sees it, the war might well have been shortened by a year or so. In the hazy twilight of a North Sea spring evening, Jellicoe had his fleet where it could force a showdown; yet he could not quite do it, partly because he knew that it

might be very risky and partly because, as Churchill remarked, Jellicoe was the one man on either side who could
have lost the entire war in one day. Jellicoe played Jutland
for a standoff. He accepted a draw, knowing that this way
he would not lose anything that could not eventually be
regained. His reasoning was flawless—except that the war
did go on for two more years, and the British Empire itself suffered because of it. As Mr. Barnett remarks, "the
last military chance of avoiding a long war and utter mutual
exhaustion had gone."

All of this is usually laid at Jellicoe's door, but Mr. Barnett thinks it goes deeper. He insists: "Jutland proves that
the spectacular collapse of British power and British industrial vigour after 1945 was not a sudden disaster due, as comforting legend has it, to the sale of overseas investments in
1914–18 and 1939–45, but the final acute phase of seventy
years of decline. For the principal armed service of a country . . . is an extension, a reflection, of that country's whole
society, and especially of its dominating groups. . . .

"Two things caused the decadence of British maritime
power: the long peaceful supremacy after Trafalgar and the
capture of the navy by that hierarchy of birth and class that
controlled so many of Britain's national institutions. . . .
The navy reflected social rather than functional values, pre-
occupation with tradition rather than technology."

It does not do to blame Jellicoe. Let the author sum it up:

"Jutland was one of the critical battles of history; it
marked the opening of that final phase of British world
power and maritime supremacy that was to end in 1945,
with the British battle fleet no more than 'Task Force 77' in
the United States Pacific Fleet, and Britain herself reduced
to financial dependency. Yet it was partly owing to Jellicoe's
personal skill as an admiral that the final collapse of British
sea power was delayed until 1945 and after."

One of the great problems men like Jellicoe faced was that
they were commanders depending in the last analysis on

the machines they controlled; and the magnificent dreadnought, the ponderous battleship on which both navies relied
at Jutland, turns out on analysis to have been one of the
oddest, most sadly flawed mechanisms ever devised by
man. It was a terribly expensive, cumbersome, and awe-
inspiring instrument of war that was actually obsolescent
when it was born and that was never able to do the things
its inventors thought it could do because of a simple but
rather frightening truth: to any purely mechanistic inven-
tion, a mechanistic answer will be devised before the inven-
tion itself can develop its potentialities.

An absorbing study of this strange instrument of naval
warfare is available in Richard Hough's *Dreadnought: A
History of the Modern Battleship,* which traces the development of this man-made dinosaur from birth to death. The
story after all is fairly short. The dreadnought—that is, the
all-big-gun battleship, heavily armored in the belief that it
would be unsinkable, and heavily armed in the hope that it
could sink all of its foes—had a life of just half a century: a
few years more than the life of the monitor, or the steam-
driven ram, and a great deal less than the life of the galley.

The dreadnought came into existence in 1906 as the cul-
mination of naval men's attempts to devise an impregnable
platform for irresistible guns. It was a battleship unlike all
previous battleships in that all of its main guns were *big:*
H.M.S. *Dreadnought* mounted ten 12-inch guns, with a bat-
tery of light guns to ward off enemy torpedo craft; it was
armored so that no guns any smaller than its own could hurt
it materially. Once it was launched, every naval power on
earth hastened to copy it. It sent all earlier battleships to the
scrap heap, and within six years the navies of the world had
forty-seven ships of this type in commission, with sixty-three
more under construction.

---

* *Dreadnought: A History of the Modern Battleship,* by Richard Hough,
with an introduction by C. S. Forester. The Macmillan Company. 268
pp. Illustrated.

The only trouble with all of this, as Mr. Hough remarks, was that the dreadnought was simply a gun platform, and the gun itself was going out of date. The big gun, of 12- or 14- or 16-inch caliber, was meant to be a ship-killer, and under ordinary circumstances that is what it was; unhappily, better ship-killers were being brought out. The torpedo was beginning to emerge as the one weapon no ship could cope with. Mines, torpedo boats, destroyers, long-range submarines, airplanes—even before the 1914 war started there were perceptive naval officers (including a number of smart juniors in the British service) who were beginning to feel that these fearfully expensive battleships were rapidly becoming obsolete because much less expensive craft could destroy them.

The real basis for Jellicoe's crippling caution at Jutland was his realization of this fact. He had enough of a numerical advantage over the German fleet to stand up against it in head-on combat, even though his foes did have a superiority, ship for ship, but he did not dare expose his irreplaceable fleet to the mines and torpedoes which the Germans might use against him. The fact that he greatly overestimated the ability of a retreating battle fleet to sow mines in its wake and also overestimated the effectiveness of torpedo attacks in that particular stage of naval development does not mean that he was wrong. He recognized one point clearly enough: it did not take a battleship to destroy a battleship. Mr. Hough points out that in all the First World War, "not one Dreadnought battleship was to be sunk by the guns of another."

Furthermore, the big-gun ship was infernally cumbersome. At Jutland, Jellicoe was in command of a fleet that extended over seven miles when it was drawn up in line of battle. It was simply too big, too long, too much the prey of faulty communications (like Moltke's army in France) to be wielded as an effective instrument. It was irresistible, in a way, but it was also extremely vulnerable. All of the nation's hopes were riding on it: inevitably, the admirals had to feel that "behind every calculation, every decision, every signal, every turn of the helm was the deeply held conviction that the disaster of defeat must always be greater than the rewards of victory." The ships, the squadrons, and the fleet must be preserved, even if the price of preserving them was victory itself. The chief function of the dreadnought, in the last analysis, was to stay afloat.

The battleship, in short, did not pay its way in World War I. In the next war it did, in a way, because by this time it had subsided to a subordinate role. It was extremely useful as an instrument for bombarding shore fortifications and as a guardian for airplane carriers, but it was no longer dominant. Mr. Hough points out, properly enough, that "where command of the air helped to grant command of the ocean's surface, the battleship performed usefully; scarcely ever in the role for which it was once devised, but very often to good purpose. When command of the air was lost—as, say, at Pearl Harbor to the Japanese and at Leyte Gulf to the Americans—then the battleship succumbed."

All of this, to be sure, is matter of common knowledge. The point is that the dreadnought was devised as an unlimited weapon, and was unable to be that even in its early days because newer weapons were available. Perhaps Jellicoe's greatest problem—the one neither he nor anyone else could have solved—was simply the fact that the dreadnought battleship, the most ponderous weapon man had ever invented, was just not up to the kind of victory he was supposed to win.

# The Dreadful Noise*

## April 1967

A man who tried to play the violin in public without study-
ing the rules of music and the techniques of musicianship
would of course need to have his head examined. (He would
also need to be silenced, but that would come automatically.) Not even in this permissive age would anyone argue
that the simple desire to produce pleasing sounds could make
up for a total lack of craftsmanship, because it is so obvious
that without craftsmanship the sounds would not be pleasing.

In other words, there are rules that have to be observed
by anyone who wants to make music. These rules are rigid,
the student has to work within their limits, and he cannot
do it unless he knows what the rules are and what they require of him. He may be able to whistle a tune acceptably
without this knowledge, but if he wants to go further he
must prepare himself. The violin is a marvelously flexible
and expressive instrument, but when it is badly handled it
makes a dreadful noise.

What is true of the violin is also true of the English language. You can do almost anything you want to do with it

* *American Heritage* magazine, April 1967

if you know how to handle it, but there are rules to be observed. Some of them seem arbitrary, and learning to work with them can be a great deal of trouble, but to go ahead without even knowing what they are and why they exist is dangerous. In trying to produce persuasive prose, the writer is likely to commit an atrocity.

This to be sure would not be worth saying, except that so many educators nowadays are arguing that the rules no longer exist. If you can speak the language, we are told, you can write it: go ahead boldly with never a backward glance, and if you make a hash out of grammar and syntax nobody will notice. The fact that by doing this you lose first clarity and then meaning itself is probably beside the point.

That is why *Modern American Usage: A Guide,** by the late Wilson Follett, is such a welcome and important book. I wish that anyone who ever tries to write anything more consequential than a letter to his family might be required to read it, to reread it, and to meditate upon it. Here is a wise, effective, and pleasingly witty attack on sloppy writing and on the things that cause sloppy writing.

Mr. Follett, unfortunately, died before the manuscript was finished. It was edited and completed by Jacques Barzun, with the assistance of some able collaborators, and it is altogether excellent.

Mr. Follett begins with the idea that the noise the violin makes ought not to be dreadful. As he puts it: ". . . there is a right way to use words and construct sentences, and many wrong ways. The right way is believed to be clearer, simpler, more logical, and hence more likely to prevent error and confusion. Good writing is easier to read; it offers a pleasant combination of sound and sense."

This seems indisputable; but hear Mr. Follett:

* *Modern American Usage: A Guide,* by Wilson Follett, edited and completed by Jacques Barzun, in collaboration with Carlos Baker, Frederick W. Dupee, Dudley Fitts, James D. Hart, Phyllis McGinley, and Lionel Trilling. Hill & Wang, Inc. 436 pp.

Against this majority view is the doctrine of an embattled minority, who make up for their small number by their great learning and their place of authority in the school system and the world of scholarship. They are the professional linguists, who deny that there is such a thing as correctness. The language, they say, is what anybody and everybody speaks. Hence there must be no interference with what they regard as a product of nature; they denounce all attempts at guiding choice; their governing principle is epitomized in the title of a speech by a distinguished member of the profession: "Can Native Speakers of a Language Make Mistakes?"

Well, they can, and do; and Mr. Follett demands "the increasingly obvious and imperative reform—a resumption in our schools of the teaching of grammar and the reading of books." What the writer needs most, he believes, is "the blessing of an orderly mind," because "for all who speak or write, the road to effective language is thinking straight." What you write reflects what you think, and if your writing is fuzzy your thinking is probably fuzzy. But old-style grammar is out of date. We used to believe that any good sentence can be parsed; that is, "it can be broken down into subjects and objects and antecedents, cases and parts of speech, modes and tenses." To do this is a lot of trouble, of course, and I can remember weary hours spent as a grade-school inmate—come to think of it, we used to say "grammar school"—parsing sentences, building intricate sentence-structure diagrams to show subject, predicate, modifying clause, and what not. It was a great bore, and I would have preferred to go fishing, but it was part of the process of learning the rules: "English does have a structure, a logic at its center, a set of principles, a consistency matching that of the orderly mind. Of this structure grammar is the working diagram and teachable plan—reason enough why, to the worker in prose, grammar remains indispensable."

All of this is very good, but it seems to me that the real riches of this book are found in its lexicon, which constitutes about seven eighths of the text. A few samples may suffice:

> Few periods in history have been so reluctant to call things by their right names as our own. Our neighbors do not go crazy, they *become disturbed;* employers no longer fire or discharge employees, they *effect a separation or termination.* Even important warnings come wrapped in cotton wool, not to say couched in falsehoods—witness this printed card put in the bedrooms of a first-class hotel: *For your added comfort and convenience please lock your door and adjust chain before retiring.*

Why, asks Mr. Follett, does it not simply say, "For your safety," and tell you to "fasten" the chain?

The lexicon points out that there are pitfalls from which only a solid knowledge of language and grammar will protect us. There is, for instance, the misuse of *like*—as in the well-known example of the cigarette advertisement. The trouble here is that "the grammatically scared" refuse to use *like* when they ought to use it. As the book points out, "When we ought to write *The Greenland birds, like the mallards, remain in the country in winter,* we must not be done out of *like* by terror lest someone suspect us of meaning *remain . . . in winter like the mallards do.*" Even worse, perhaps, is the misuse—or the timid failure to use—the objective form of the pronoun *who:* "Between those who are afraid of sounding ignorant and those who are afraid of sounding superior, *whom* falls into comparative disuse and causes increasing discomfort in its users." Thus we get such locutions as *I know perfectly well whom you are,* where the writer thinks *whom* is the object of *know* when it is really the subject of *are;* and a sentence reading *Ahead of them on the None-such road they descried Lord Grey de Hilton, whom Essex declared was his enemy.* Mr. Follett's comment here is satisfactory: "One of the paradoxes of the time is that some liberal grammarians who are implacable toward *whom* in its orthodox uses will tie themselves into knots in the effort to condone *whom* in this particular construction. Apparently they have a feeling that it ought to command the blessing of the learned because it tramples on prescriptive grammar."

Then there is the terribly abused word *disinterested.* Maybe the battle here has been lost, but the writers of this book are not ready to give up. Thus:

> *Disinterest,* or *disinterestedness,* as it is now employed by the careless or the desperate, not only blurs the meaning but also stops the reader who can see two possible meanings, because it is still the name of a great, sterling, and positive virtue—freedom from self-seeking motives. It is not the name of a lack, which is what the writer was looking for. *Is one of the consequences of good times a disinterest in bad news?* Here *disinterest* is the wrong word, *uninterestedness* would be a fumbling one. *Indifference* (with *to*) is the inevitable word.

The temptation to go on quoting until closing time is strong, but there are limits. The point I want to make is that this book is an excellent corrective for the sloppiness, imprecision, and frequent unintelligibility of much that passes for writing these days. The English language is one of the most flexible instruments man has devised. Used properly, it can say anything the user wants to say. It cannot be used properly unless one knows something about the governing rules and principles. Although Mr. Follett pours out his scorn on the educationalist's misuse of the word *discipline,* grammar does constitute a *discipline,* in the literal sense, and it is time writers began subjecting themselves to it.

# The Great American Game*

## April 1959

By the carefully repeated definition of men who stand to make money out of its acceptance, baseball is the Great American Game. The expression was invented long ago and it has been rammed home by talented press agents ever since, even in times when most Americans seemed to be interested very largely in something else. But what has given the phrase its sticking power is not the fact that a big industry has kept plugging it, or the allied fact that unceasing repetition has dinned it into an unreflecting public's ears for generations, but simply the fact that in its underlying essence it is perfectly true.

Baseball is the American game, great or otherwise, because it reflects so perfectly certain aspects of the American character that no other sport quite portrays.

It has few of the elements of pure sportsmanship, as that dubious word is commonly accepted, and it is not notably a game for gentlemen. But it does embody certain native-born fundamentals, including above all others the notion that the big thing about any contest is to win it. It also is built upon the idea that anything you can get away with is permissible, and it is the only sport (at least the only one since

* *American Heritage* magazine, April 1959

the Roman populace sat in the thumbs-down section at the gladiatorial games) that puts an invitation to homicide in one of its enduring sayings: "Kill the umpire!" (The thing has actually been attempted, too, more than once.) It is pre-eminently the sport for the professional rather than for the amateur, the sport in which the well-intentioned duffer neither is given nor especially wants a part.

Almost everyone in the country has played it at one time or another, but almost nobody except the professional dreams of going on playing it once full manhood has come. It is a spectator sport in which each spectator has had just enough personal experience to count himself an expert, and it is the only pastime on earth that leans heavily on the accumulation of page upon page of inherently dry statistics. It is also an unchanging pageant and a ritualized drama, as completely formalized as the Spanish bullfight, and although it is wholly urbanized it still speaks of the small town and the simple, rural era that lived before the automobile came in to blight the landscape. One reason for this is that in a land of unending change, baseball changes very little. There has been no important modification of its rules for well over half a century. The ball in use now will go farther when properly hit, and the gloves worn on defense are designed to do automatically what personal skill once had to do, but aside from these things the game is as it was in the early 1900s. Even the advent of night baseball, which seemed like pure sacrilege when it was introduced two decades ago, has made little difference; the pictorial aspect of the game— which is one of its most important features—has perhaps even gained thereby. The neat green field looks greener and cleaner under the lights, the moving players are silhouetted more sharply, and the enduring visual fascination of the game—the immobile pattern of nine men, grouped according to ancient formula and then, suddenly, to the sound of a wooden bat whacking a round ball, breaking into swift ritualized movement, movement so standardized that even the tyro in the bleachers can tell when someone goes off in the wrong direction—this is as it was in the old days. A gaffer from the era of William McKinley, abruptly brought back to the second half of the twentieth century, would find very little in modern life that would not seem new, strange, and rather bewildering, but put in a good grandstand seat back of first base he would see nothing that was not completely familiar.

But that is only the surface part of it. Baseball, highly organized, professionalized within an inch of its life, and conducted by men who like dollars better than they like sport, still speaks for the old days when nine young men in an open park somehow expressed the hot competitive instincts of everybody and spoke for home-town pride.

And perhaps the central part of all of this is the fact that in its essence baseball is still faintly disreputable and rowdy. Its players chew tobacco, or at least look as if they were chewing it; many of them do not shave every day; and they argue bitterly with each other, with their opponents, and with the umpires just as they did when John McGraw and Ed Delehanty were popular idols. They have borrowed nothing from the "sportsmanship" of more sedate countries; they believe that when you get into a fight you had better win, and the method by which you win does not matter very much. Anything goes; victory is what counts.

This John McGraw, for example. When he was playing third base and there was a runner there, and someone hit a fly to the outfield, McGraw would unobtrusively hook his fingers in the player's belt so that the take-off for the plate, once the ball was caught, would be delayed by half a second or so. He got away with it, too, and no one thought the worse of him, until one day a baserunner unbuckled his belt in this situation and, legging it for home, left the belt dangling in McGraw's hand, tangible evidence of crime. Note, also, that baseball knows about the bean ball—the ball thrown at the batter's head to drive him away from the plate and hamper his hitting process. A big leaguer was once killed by such a pitch; it has been condemned by everybody ever since then, and it is still a regular feature of the game.

In its essentials, then, baseball is plebeian, down-to-earth, and robustious. Even half a century ago it was dwindling to the rank of secondary sport in the colleges. Professors who have adjusted themselves to the presence on the campus of *soi-disant* students who are paid to attend college so that they may play football have a way of considering the football player one cut above the baseball player. The former may be a hulking behemoth of pure muscle, wholly incapable of differentiating between Virgil's *Eclogues* and Boyle's law, but he does not seem quite as uncouth as the baseball player —who, in his own turn, may also be on the campus as a paid hand, the difference being that he is being paid by some major-league team that wants to see his athletic skills developed, while the football player gets his from ardent alumni who want to see the college team beat State on Homecoming Day next fall. There has never been any social cachet attached to skill on the diamond.

The reason, obviously, is that baseball came up from the sand lots—the small town, the city slum, and the like. It had a rowdy air because rowdies played it. One of the stock tableaux in American sports history is the aggrieved baseball player jawing with the umpire. In all our games, this tableau is unique; it belongs to baseball, from the earliest days it has been an integral part of the game, and even in the carefully policed major leagues today it remains unchanged. Baseball never developed any of the social niceties.

In the old days, when (as we suppose, anyway) most of us lived in small towns, or at least in fairly small cities, the local baseball team represented civic pride, to say nothing of representing at the same time the dreams of a great many young men who wished to be much more athletic than they actually were. In very small towns, its games were usually held in Farmer Jones's pasture, where the difficulty, in a hot moment of split-second play, of distinguishing between third base and some natural cow-pasture obstacle sometimes led to odd happenings; and in slightly larger places the county fairground or a recreational park at the end of the streetcar line provided the arena. In any case, muscular young men, wearing the singularly unbecoming uniforms that were standardized 75 years ago, presently took their positions on the grass, and the game was on.

It was, and still is, hotly competitive, and within reasonable limits anything goes. If the umpire (there was just one, in the old days) could be suborned to give all vital judgments in favor of the home side, all well and good; no one ever blushed to accept a victory that derived from an umpire's bias. If he could be intimidated, so that close decisions would go as the spectators wanted them to go, that also was good. This often happened; an umpire who decided a crucial play against the home team was quite likely to be mobbed, and few pictures from the old-time sports album are more authentic or more enduring than the vision of an umpire frantically legging it for the train, pursued by irate citizens who wished to do him great bodily harm. It took physical courage to render impartial judgments in old-time small-town baseball, and not all umpires were quite up to it.

If the umpire could be deceived while the game was on, that also was good. A man running from first to third on a base hit would cut twenty feet short of second base if he thought he could get away with it, and no one dreamed of censuring him for it. If an opposing player could be intimidated, so that he shirked his task, that was good, too. Not for nothing was the greatest baseball player who ever lived, Ty Cobb, famous for sitting on the bench just before the game sharpening his spikes with a file. An infielder, witnessing this, and knowing that Cobb was practically certain to ram those spikes into his calf or thigh in a close play, was apt to flinch just a little at the moment of contact, and out of that split second of withdrawal Cobb would gain the hair's edge of advantage that he needed. It was considered fair, too, to denounce an opponent verbally, with any sort of profane, personal objurgation that came to mind, on the off-chance that he might become unsettled and do less than his best. (This still goes on, like practically all of the other traditional things in baseball, and the "bench jockey"—the man who will say anything at all if he thinks it will upset an enemy's poise—can be a prized member of a big-league team even now.)

Baseball is conservative. What was good enough in Cap Anson's day is good enough now, and a populace that could stand unmoved while the federal Constitution was amended would protest with vehemence at any tampering with the formalities of baseball. It looks as it used to look; the batter still grabs a handful of dust between swings, the catcher still slams the ball over to third base after a strike-out, and the umpire still jerks thumb over right shoulder to indicate a put-out. (Dismayingly enough, some umpires now grossly exaggerate this gesture, using an elaborate full-arm swing, but possibly the point is a minor one.)

An inning begins; the pitcher takes his warm-up tosses, now as in the days half a century ago, and after three, four, or five of these he steps aside and the catcher whips the ball down to second base. The second baseman tosses it to the shortstop, two yards away, and the shortstop throws it to the third baseman, who is standing halfway between his own base and the pitcher's box; the third baseman, in turn, tosses it over to the pitcher, and the inning can get started. To vary from this formula is unthinkable; from the little leaguers up to Yankee Stadium, it is as one with the laws of the Medes and the Persians.

Then action: players shifting about, pounding their gloves, uttering cries of encouragement (which, like all the rest, are verbatim out of the script of 1900); and the batter approaches the plate, swinging two bats (another ironclad requirement), tossing one aside, planting his feet in the batter's box, and then swinging his single bat in determined menace. The fielders slowly freeze into fixed positions; for a moment no one anywhere moves, except that the pitcher goes into his stretch, takes a last look around, and then delivers—and then the frozen pattern breaks, the ball streaks off, men move deftly from here to there, and the quick moments of action are on.

In all of this there is unending fascination, coupled with the knowledge that wholly fantastic athletic feats may at any moment be displayed by any one of the players. Even an easy fly ball to the outfield or a simple grounder to short can call forth a nonchalant, effortless expertness that a man from another land would find quite incredible. (I once took an Englishman to see his first baseball game, and he was dumfounded by the simplest plays, marveling at what all the rest of us took for automatic outs.) In no contest can the split second be so important. A routine double play can make both outs with no more than half a second to spare, and if the half second is lost anywhere, the player who lost it will be derided for a clumsy oaf.

Primarily a team game, baseball is also the game for the individualist. The team play is essential, and when you watch closely you can see it, but the focus is usually on one man. A baserunner streaks for second with the pitch, falls away while in full stride, and slides in in a cloud of dust, baseman stabbing at him with gloved hand, umpire bending to peer through the murk and call the play; an outfielder runs deep and far, arching ball coming down—apparently —just out of his reach, trajectories of fielder and baseball coming miraculously together at the last, gloved hand going out incredibly to pick the ball out of the air; a pitcher who has been getting his lumps looks about at filled bases, glowers at the batter, and then sends one in that is struck at and missed . . . always, some individual is trying for an astounding feat of athletic prowess and, now and then, actually accomplishing it.

Hence baseball celebrates the vicarious triumph. The spectator can identify himself completely with the player, and the epochal feat becomes, somehow, an achievement of his own. Babe Ruth, mocking the Chicago Cubs, pointing to the distant bleachers and then calmly hitting the ball into those bleachers, took a host of Walter Mittys with him when he jogged around the bases. (There is some dispute about this, to be sure; he was jawing with the Cubs, but purists say he did not actually call his shot. This makes no difference whatever.) It was the same when old Grover Cleveland Alexander, the all-but-washed-up veteran of many baseball wars, came into the seventh inning of a decisive World Series game, found the bases filled with Yankees, and struck out Tony Lazzeri, going on to win game and Series; and this was after a wearing night on the tiles, Alexander having supposed that his work was over until next spring. Many an aging fan shared in Old Alex's triumph.

These things are part of baseball's legend, for the game never forgets its gallery of immortals. That it actually has a tangible Hall of Fame, with bronze plaques to commemorate the greatest, is only part of the story; the noble deeds of the super-players are handed down in bar-side stories, year after year, losing nothing in the telling. Some of the heroes have been supermen, in a way, at that. There was, for instance, Shoeless Joe Jackson, barred from baseball in mid-career because he let himself be bribed to help lose a World Series. (He did not do very well at losing; even under a bribe, he batted .375 in that Series—a natural hitter who just couldn't make himself miss even when paid to do so.) A sand-lot pitcher tells of a day, a whole generation later, when, pitching for a textile-mill team in the Carolinas, he found on the opposing team none other than Jackson—a pathetic, fat, doddering wreck in his late fifties, with a monstrous belly like some disreputable Santa Claus, still picking up a few odd bucks playing semi-pro ball under an assumed name. The young pitcher figured Jackson would be easy; a low inside curve, coming in close to the overhang of that prodigious paunch, was obviously the thing to throw. He threw, Jackson swung, and swung as he used to thirty years earlier, and the ball went far out of the park, one of the most authoritative home runs the young pitcher ever witnessed. Old Jackson lumbered heavily around the bases, and halfway between third and home he turned to accost the young pitcher. "Son," he said, "I always could hit them low inside curves."

There were others cast in similar molds. . . . Rube Waddell, the wholly legendary character who, when cold sober, which was not often, may have been the greatest pitcher of them all: the man who now and then, on a whim, would gesture the entire outfield off the premises and then retire the side without visible means of support; Walter Johnson, who once pitched fifty-odd consecutive scoreless innings, and who to the end of his days had nothing much in his repertoire except an unhittable fast ball; Tris Speaker, who played such a short center field that he often threw a batter out at first on what ought to have been a legitimate down-the-middle base hit; and lean Satchel Paige, who in his great days in the Negro leagues had a way of pointing to the shortstop and then throwing something which the batter must hit to short, and who then would go on around the infield in the same way, compelling the opposition to hit precisely where he wanted it to hit. The legends are, in some ways, the most enduring part of the game. Baseball has even more of them than the Civil War, and its fans prize them highly.

Under the surface, baseball is always played to a subdued but inescapable tension, because at any second one of these utterly fabulous events may take place. The game may be distressingly one-sided, and the home team may come up in the ninth inning five runs behind, and in a clock game like football or basketball the margin would be physically un-

beatable; but in baseball anything can happen, and the tini-
est fluke can change everything. (Remember the World
Series game the Yankees won when a Brooklyn catcher
dropped a third strike with two men out in the ninth?) A
commonplace game can turn into a hair-raiser at any moment, and things do not actually need to happen to create
the suspense. A free-hitting, high-scoring game may be most
eventful, but few strains are greater than the strain of
watching a pitcher protect a 1–0 lead in the late innings of
a routine game. Nothing, perhaps, actually happens—but
every time the ball is thrown the game may turn upside
down, and nobody ever forgets it.

All of this is built in, for the spectator. Built in, as well, is
the close attention to records and statistics. Batting averages and pitchers' records are all-important; to know that a
Rogers Hornsby, for instance, could bat more than .400 in
three different years—that is, could average getting two hits
for every five times he came to the plate, 154 games a year,
for three years—is important. It has been suggested, now and
then, that big league playing schedules be reduced from 154
games to some smaller figure, and the suggestion has always
been howled down: it would upset all the averages. Unthinkable; how do you compare today's pitcher with Walter
Johnson or Lefty Grove if today's pitcher plays in fewer
games every year?*

The circumstances under which baseball is played nowadays have changed greatly, to be sure. Less than half a century ago, every town that amounted to anything at all was
represented in some league of professional players, and these
leagues—the minor leagues, of hallowed memory—have been
dissolving and vanishing, as more and more spectators get

---

* This paragraph was written in the 1950s, and since then the unthinkable change has taken place; the year's schedule for big league clubs now
contains more games than in the old days, and the records have gone awry.
Witness the case of Roger Maris, who broke Ruth's home run record and
got into the record book with an asterisk which puts a slight cloud on his
achievement.

their games by television or by radio and ignore the local ball park. The Little Leagues have come up, and semi-subsidized sand-lot leagues, and even college baseball is here and there enjoying a new lease on life—after all, the new players in the big leagues have to come from somewhere, and besides, young Americans still like to play baseball; but the old pattern is gone, and even the major leagues themselves have undergone profound changes and, to a purist from the old days, are all but unrecognizable. Where are the St. Louis Browns, or the Philadelphia Athletics, or the Boston Braves—or, for the matter of that, even the magnificent New York Giants, and the Brooklyn Dodgers? Gone forever, to be sure, with new cities taking over, and with a few old-timers muttering that the last days are at hand.

Actually, the last days are probably a long, long way off, for baseball even in its modern guise has not changed in its essentials. It is a rough, tough game, encased by rules that were made to be broken if the breaking can be accomplished smoothly enough, a game that never quite became entirely respectable, a game in which nobody wants to do anything but win. It will undoubtedly be around for a good time to come, and it will continue, in spite of its own press agents, to be in truth the great American game.

Or so, at least, believes one old-time fan.

# A Historical Afterword*

## 1964

The exact and complete truth about any tragic historic event
is almost impossible to get. We can never know precisely
how and why certain things happened. The best we can do,
usually, is to work out a rough approximation—to say, somewhere within these boundaries lies a truth that we shall
never really see; somehow, out of all of these facts, this
result emerged. Even the most painstaking history is a bridge
across an eternal mystery.

This is so even when the event in question took place in
the limelight, with everybody watching. Perhaps it is especially so then. Too many people see too much and nobody
has time to cross-examine them. Facts get entangled with
rumors, imagination adds its own touches, and when the
historian tries to see the tragedy he has to study it through
a haze of myth and legend.

For an example, there was the assassination of President
Abraham Lincoln, which took place in a packed theater before hundreds of possible eyewitnesses, and which is still
wrapped in so many uncertainties that some of its most fan-

* THE OFFICIAL WARREN COMMISSION REPORT on the
ASSASSINATION of PRESIDENT JOHN F. KENNEDY, Doubleday
& Company, Inc. 1964

tastic legends are items of very recent development. For another, there is the assassination of President John F. Kennedy, which was accompanied by full coverage of press, newsreels and television and which began to develop its own legends before the body of the murdered man had even been laid to rest.

One trouble is that things actually seen get mixed up with things imagined, deduced or suspected. Another is that facts disappear as time passes; men die, records vanish, things said are forgotten, and the chance to know is diminished. Painstaking deduction and study can separate much of the unreal from the real and cover some of the gaps, to be sure, but in the end we still have to take a great deal on faith. The area of genuine certainty becomes very narrow.

A further trouble is that when we reach that area of certainty we are at a point of departure rather than the end of our quest. To find out what the facts are can be hard enough: to find out what they mean can be ever so much harder. We have to explore the relationship of intangibles. We try to appraise the spirit of a time and the climate of a place, and when we think we have done that we have to go on and see what effect the spirit and climate had—if indeed they had any effect at all—on the specific thing that happened in that time and place. Doing this, we follow a path that is full of pitfalls.

But the facts come first. Any historian who confronts a gap in the record of bygone days knows moments of despair when he complains bitterly that no one took the trouble to dig out and assemble all of the facts while those facts were still available. To use unlimited resources in order to make a record for history, a record as broad and as all-inclusive as it possibly can be, to do it while everything is still fresh, and to do it with no other earthly motive than a desire to establish the full truth—this is the sort of thing that only governments can do, and they almost never dream of doing it. A complete and reliable account of the actual facts sur-

rounding any historic tragedy is all but impossible to come
by.

That is why this report of the Warren Commission is so
important.

Here, for the first time, a government moved promptly
to get all of the facts on the record. The Warren Commission
was set up and put to work immediately after President
Kennedy's assassination, and it had only one responsibility: to get at the complete truth, as far as that can be done
by fallible human beings, and to make an unvarnished report on it. The Commission was not supposed to prove anything. It had no ax to grind. Its membership, like its directive,
lifted it above suspicion. It had the task of finding out
everything it could about a shocking human tragedy and to
publish what it learned without regard to the consequences.
This task, by all indications, the Warren Commission has
accomplished, and it ought to be remembered, again, that
governments rarely try to do anything of the kind.

So here is the record: a comprehensive study of a great
and terrible moment in history, undertaken in the faith that
the myths and legends that falsify so much history would
not grow if full light was immediately shed on the dark
places.

The Warren Commission talked to everyone who could
conceivably know anything about the assassination. It enlisted the ablest professional help in existence, studied the
facts it had unearthed, put those facts together in the light
of its members' own knowledge of the law, of people and
of the national state of mind in the fall of 1963, and then
it wrote its report. The report may not have the final, complete and revealed truth about the miserable affair in Dallas—
that kind of truth is the rarest commodity on earth, and it
probably is reserved for the enlightenment that will come
to us beyond the river—but it comes as close to it as fallible
human beings can come. The best people who could be found
spent months trying to do the most honest job possible.

Neither the caliber of the investigators nor the motives that inspired them can be impugned by anyone above the mental age of ten. This story of the murder of President Kennedy is the most complete we are ever likely to get.

To establish the importance of this accomplishment, we might compare this assassination with that of President Lincoln, almost one century earlier.

No commission was set up in 1865 to get at all of the facts. The War Department, to be sure, made its own investigation, but its chief purpose was to prove that the President had been murdered by the same people who had recently tried by force of arms to establish the independence of the Southern Confederacy. Its investigation was literally irresponsible: it worked in the dark, it published no conclusive findings, it covered up items that tended to disprove its chosen thesis, and it muddied the waters so completely that a century later no one can be entirely sure that he knows all he needs to know about the events that led to Mr. Lincoln's death. The situation has remained so cloudy, indeed, that within the present generation supposedly responsible men have tried to show that the assassination was the result of a plot engineered by (of all people on earth) the United States Secretary of War, Edwin M. Stanton. It is of course true that no substantial historian takes this seriously, but it is also true that no one can really disprove it.

It is permissible to believe that the work of the Warren Commission has saved future generations from that kind of nonsense. Here, to repeat, is the record, compiled and studied while it was still fresh by men of stature who were not trying to prove any thesis at all. The myths and legends which so often go to make a fable out of history will have a hard time putting down any roots here.

Yet when all of this has been said, and emphasized, it remains true that the story of President Kennedy's death shares one thing with the story of the death of President

Lincoln: it leaves us with the uneasy feeling that there are some things about it that we shall never really know. We have the facts, but beyond them there is an emptiness in which we can see nothing but the shadows of our own fears and suspicions.

There is a subtle difference between these two cases. President Lincoln lived in a time of intense anger and hatred. He was killed by a crackpot fanatic who was obviously motivated by the atmosphere of civil war, and even though John Wilkes Booth was self-inspired and acted by no man's bidding, it is difficult to see the murder of President Lincoln as anything else than the natural result of a time when men's emotions had gone out of control. Booth served neither Edwin M. Stanton nor Jefferson Davis, but the heated, supercharged climate of his era did somehow bring him to the point of explosive violence. We still lack many of the facts about the Lincoln assassination, but we know what the whole terrible business meant. American society was fevered to the point of delirium in the Civil War, and Booth's mad act was the logical final spasm of violence. Given the four years that had just ended, something like this was bound to happen. The tragedy in Ford's Theatre was as much a part of the war fury as Chickamauga or Spotsylvania Courthouse.

In the case of President Kennedy we have the hard facts but we do not quite know what they mean. How far was Lee Oswald like John Wilkes Booth? Did his haunted mind, like Booth's, somehow respond to the hatreds and terrors that boiled up all around him, or did it simply respond to some marsh fire that only he could see? Was his act part of 1963 in the sense that Booth's was part of 1865, or was it simply an irrational explosion that might have happened to any President at any time and in any place? The Warren Commission could find no trace of a plot that used Oswald as trigger man. It saw no evidence of a conspiracy of either the right or the left. It established that truth, which cuts the ground out from under the myth-makers but which also leaves us confronting a riddle: What did this thing really mean?

The question will bother us for a long time to come because it involves the intangibles that lie beyond the reach of any commission. We know that John F. Kennedy was President at a time when many diverse hatreds were being aroused, hatreds born of hot war and cold war and the agonizing difficulty of adjusting a complex society to a time of incomprehensible changes; we know that he devoted himself as President to the task of quelling those hatreds and facing the future with hope and without terror; and we know that in the midst of all of this he was shot to death. There our knowledge ends. In Lincoln's case we can see that an era of irrational fury led inescapably to an irrational act of hatred. In Kennedy's case we do not know.

Perhaps we shall never know. There are mysteries in the human story. We are left with Plutarch's somber remark: ". . . so very difficult a matter is it to trace and find out the truth of anything by history." We are left with this factual record, as complete as dedicated men can make it. We can study it, searching our hearts for the answer, for generations to come.

# The Real Michigan*

## 1957

Michigan is perhaps the strangest state in the Union, a
place where the past, the present and the future are all
tied up together in a hard knot. It is the 20th Century incarnate, and if you look closely you can also see the twenty-
first coming in; but it is also the 19th Century, the backward glance and the authentic feel and taste of a day
that is gone forever. It killed the past and it is the past;
it is the skyscraper, the mass-production line and the frantic
rush into what the machine will some day make of all of us,
and at the same time it is golden sand, blue water, green
pine trees on empty hills, and a wind that comes down from
the cold spaces, scented with the forests that were
butchered by hard-handed men in checked flannel shirts
and floppy pants. It is the North Country wedded to the
force that destroyed it.

You enter Michigan, mostly, by way of Detroit, which
is something special. It is a profound weight on the land;
an enormous city, with great skyscrapers taking the light
from Canada, automobile factories and used-car lots
scattered across the flat prairies, enough business strewn

* *Holiday,* August 1957

along the Detroit River to make a Russian's eyes pop; and in the old days, which lasted until World War II, you came into Detroit, usually, by steamboat, which was an experience in itself.

The boats came up from the Lake Erie ports, Cleveland and Buffalo and Sandusky, and they gave a theatrical touch to the whole business. Lake Erie is beautiful and shallow and treacherous, with a capacity for whipping up unexpected storms that would bother any mariner who ever lived, although mostly it is pleasant enough; and the old side-wheelers came paddling down its length, usually in the middle of the night—it was nice sleeping, in a snug stateroom on one of those boats, with an air-conditioned wind coming in at the open porthole, and the wash of the paddle wheels beating a quiet rhythm in the darkness—and in the morning the boat came up the Detroit River, and the factories and pumping stations on the bank suddenly made you realize that man had taken over Nature and was trying to make something out of it. Then, a little after breakfast time, the boat docked along the Detroit water front, and no city in America offered a more thrilling or exciting entrance.

The boats are mostly gone, and this is really Detroit's fault. Detroit did not exactly invent the automobile, but it picked the thing up when it was nothing better than a costly and unreliable toy for the rich and made it a necessity for everybody in America, and the automobile—getting slightly out of hand—killed the Great Lakes passenger boats, except for a few cruise ships. You come into Detroit nowadays in your own car, or perhaps by train, and the old impact is gone. The place dawns on you gradually now; it used to hit you between the eyes, with the early light slanting in from beyond Ontario. But even now Detroit clamors at you, arrogantly, with all the confidence that comes to men who know they are really in charge of things and who don't mind enjoying the feeling, and there is something overwhelming about it all.

For here is a foretaste of what the machine is doing to us. Here men picked up the Industrial Revolution and swung it; this place, with its infinite genius for making any sort of contrivance men have ever dreamed of, and making it more cheaply and better than anyone else, is the doorway to the future. Everything goes in a rush, everybody is busy—and the place is big and sprawling and grimy and pulsing with life. Here is where we are going, make no mistake about it, and the big financial centers down East can say what they like and be hanged. Detroit sets the pace because this is where the muscle and the knowledge are; and if you don't think the future belongs to America, you should come here and breathe the air for a while.

Detroit makes its bow to the past, of course. It has such a place as Greenfield Village, in Dearborn, and here the past that Detroit killed forever—the past of wayside inns, one-man machine shops, quiet country villages snuggling by the route of stagecoaches, and rural dancers moving to the wheezy tunes scraped out by self-taught fiddlers—is preserved like a fly in amber, and it is very much worth visiting. But this, after all, is only a gesture. Detroit has been taking us away from that for half a century, and if it shows you Greenfield Village it also shows you the machine-age pace which turned everything Dearborn has on exhibit into museum pieces. Dearborn houses both this fragment of the past and also the Ford Motor Company, which did as much as any one organism could do to put the past in its place.

Detroit's streets come in like the spokes of a wheel, the other half of the wheel having been cut off by the Detroit River. Because the pace has been uneven there are vast skyscrapers standing beside parking lots, with rummy old brick buildings from the Civil War era snuggling up against twenty-story hotels and elongated office buildings; burlesque theaters and sleazy secondhand-book stores rub elbows with the most up-to-date, chromium-and-cutstone buildings that America can build, and the river drifts by, down in front, bearing the iron ore and coal and petroleum on which modern America is built; and whether you like it or not you can feel the hard pulse of America beating up and down these automobile-clogged streets.

Some years ago a civic-minded booster dreamed up the phrase, "dynamic Detroit," to express the essence of this city. He hit it off perfectly. Detroit *is* dynamic. Here is where they call the tune, and it is not a tune the Greenfield Village fiddlers ever quite managed to express.

But Detroit, after all, is not really Michigan. Its industrial empire spraddles over a good part of the state, to be sure—with Flint, and Pontiac, and Jackson and Lansing and Grand Rapids and all the rest—but the tremendous industrial nexus centered here is only half of the story. The other half is something very different—old times, the breath of bygone days and memories that went out of date before the men who remembered them were old—and as a man born out of his proper time I love this other Michigan a good deal more than I love Detroit.

The map of the Lower Peninsula of Michigan is shaped like a fat old-fashioned mitten—a left-hand mitten, placed palm down, with a bulky thumb sticking out into the cold blue of Lake Huron. Detroit is down in the lower right-hand margin, below where the thumb begins, and the great industrial network lies across the lower part of the state: across the upper part of the wrist. But if you will take the map, and draw a line from Bay City—at the bottom of the gap between the bulbous thumb and the rest of the hand —straight west across the state, you will have cut Michigan into its two distinctive parts. Everything below the line is 20th Century; everything above it is North Country—old, half empty, touched by the cold winds that drift down from the Arctic, with trees and sand and crystal-clear water and drowsy small towns as its distinguishing marks. It is a country that will put its seal on you if you are not careful, because it offers a lonely beauty and an escape from almost everything Detroit stands for.

The present falls away, when you go up into this part of the state. Suppose you drive up from Detroit, along U. S. Route 10; it goes through places like Flint and Saginaw and Midland, any one of which would be world-famous if it were in some other country—and then, suddenly, it takes you into the empty cut-over land, where ghost towns cluster by the road, where the rivers flow cold and clear past hills that furnished lumber for half the world a generation or two ago, where cabins nestle down by quiet lakes and where the air drifts straight through you as if nobody had ever soiled it with smoke or grime or gas fumes. From here on north there are not so many farms, the soil is very sandy, excellent for growing pine trees, not often so good for growing anything else, and if it amuses you to count abandoned farms (unpainted shacks going peacefully to ruin amid fields nobody has tilled for a quarter century or more) you can make quite a list in an afternoon's drive. The road leads you out of ambition into peace and contentment; the deceptive light of an eternal summer afternoon lies on the rolling country; the innumerable lakes glitter brightly blue in the fading light, and when you stop your car and listen you hear a blessed quiet.

This part of the state must have been quite a sight, a hundred years ago. Over an area of better than 25,000 square miles there was a magnificent forest—great pines, mostly, with a healthy sprinkling of hardwoods like maples and beeches—like nothing you can find in America today. From lake to lake and for 250 miles from north to south there was an eternal green twilight, with open spaces where the lakes and rivers were; twilight, with the wind forever making an unobtrusive noise in the branches overhead, brown matted needles and leaves underfoot—everything just about as it was shortly after the last ice age.

There is one tiny fragment of it left. If you will go to the little town of Kalkaska, in the northwest part of the state's Lower Peninsula, and drive thirty miles or so to the east, you will reach Hartwick Pines State Park; and here, running down to the bank of the Au Sable River, is an eighty-five-acre tract of virgin timber, the last that remains, preserved for tourists. You leave your car by the park-administration building and suddenly you are in the middle of it, with trees rising 150 feet overhead, and a shaded coolness all about that is proof against the summer's worst heat wave. Walking through it is not unlike walking through a cathedral. It has that effect on people. It is even more moving in the dead of winter, with the big trees coming up out of a white silence that is all but absolute; the trouble is that then you have to use skis or snowshoes to get there.

Anyway, Michigan a century ago was one magnificent forest, and even as recently as the Civil War it had hardly been touched. But then the lumberjacks went to work, and they shaved the countryside the way a razor shaves a man's chin. Where there had been wilderness, boom lumber towns sprang up, with rickety railroad lines threading their way back into the hills. In the springtime, every stream was clogged with logs, with lumberjacks scampering across the treacherous shifting carpet with peavy and cant hook, mounds of sawdust rising beside the busy mills, and a mill town with 1200 inhabitants normally supported from twelve to twenty saloons. Michigan voted for prohibition before the Federal prohibition amendment went into effect in 1920, and anyone who remembers what those saloons did to small-town life can easily understand why. For a time Saginaw was the greatest lumber city in the world, then Muskegon had the title, and then some other place; fresh-cut boards were stacked in endless piles by the railroad sidings or the lakeside wharves . . . and then, all of a sudden, it was all over. The lumber was gone, the mills were dismantled, the booming cities and towns lapsed into drowsiness, store-fronts were boarded up—and the razor which had done all of this shaving had left a stubble of stumps like a frowsy three-day beard across thousands of square miles. Some towns died entirely, some almost died, and the endless whine of the gang saws became quiet forever.

All of which put its mark on a whole generation of people. Here was a region half the size of Ireland which, after only fifty years of history, suddenly found itself at a dead end. A society began to decay before it had matured. Towns dwindled and died before the eyes of the very men who had founded them. Boys who grew to manhood in these dying towns moved off to the city, leaving behind the old folks and the girls—half a century ago it was not so simple for an untrained girl to make a place for herself in a faroff city, and thousands upon thousands of these girls were condemned to lives of unwanted loneliness. They were strong and healthy and they had dreams and high hopes, and these came to very little because life had shoved them off into a side alley, since marriage was just about the only career a girl could hope for in those days. The human cost of a dying boom can be pretty high.

So they killed the infinite forest, once and for all. But there was still the land itself, rolling in vast gentle waves under a clear blue sky; there were the hundreds and hundreds of lakes, blue and cold and sparkling with imitation whitecaps; there was the great stretch of sand, putting a golden border on the water; there were the rivers, so clear you could count bits of gravel ten feet deep, so cold they turned your feet numb if you tried to wade; and there was the air, filtered by its eternal drift down from the ultimate edge of icy nowhere, fresh enough to revive a Peruvian mummy, odorous with the scent of jack pines.

All of this adds up to an earthly paradise for people from the hot cities who want to get away from asphalt and noise and muggy heat when they have a chance and touch base with Mother Nature; and today the tourist trade is the second industry in the entire state, topped only by the exalted automobile industry itself. This place where the wilderness used to be may indeed be the North Country, but it is only a hop-skip-and-jump from enormous centers of population. From Detroit or Chicago, it is a handy one-day drive to any spot in the Lower Peninsula, but at the end of the drive you feel that you have left the city and all of its works in another world.

So the old lumber area has had a rebirth, and the air of defeat and decline has vanished. This change has gone hand in hand with others. For one thing, the trees are coming back; huge state and national forests lie across vast stretches of empty land. In addition, there is a belt of cherry and peach orchards twenty miles wide and 200 miles long down the western side of the state. In spring, when the blossoms are out, the rolling hillsides near Lake Michigan offer a spectacle of breath-taking beauty, and many a town that used to live on its sawmills now lives on its cannery-and-packing plant. Every spring they have a big "cherry festival" at Traverse City—a bright, bustling little city which has made full recovery from the death of the lumber boom —and a pretty girl is named Cherry Queen; her function, usually, in addition to posing for photographs, is to take a cherry pie to Washington and present it to the President. This makes a nice trip for the girl, nets the President a first-rate pie, and presumably makes everybody happy.

But under everything there is this strange, beautiful, lonely land itself, this land of blue sky and clear water, where puff-ball clouds drift lazily overhead, trailing pleasant shadows over water and forest and bright little towns as if nobody ever had to be in a hurry about anything and time had come to a standstill just because what is here and now is too pleasant to leave. This is good country to come from and it is even better to go back to. It is a land of memories and also a land of escape: a place where you can be utterly idle in more pleasant ways than any other place I know.

I was born in Michigan and I grew up there, and not long ago I went back to see what it is like today. I came in through the industrial network in the lower right-hand corner of the state, and after a while I was driving northwest on U. S. Route 10—a fine road which goes for many miles at a stretch without touching a town, and which cannot in any case touch a real, full-dress city because in all of Michigan, north of that east-west line from Bay City, there is not a single place with as many as 20,000 permanent residents.

Beyond Clare, which calls itself the gateway to the northland, I turned right on M 115, which goes on past pleasant little lakes dotted with summer cottages, past a sprinkling of drowsy farms, and past uncounted miles of unused land. Yet a road, after all, takes you where you yourself are going, and not where the road goes, and what you see depends mostly on what's inside of you; and when you go back to re-explore your own country you are likely to find memories and dreams all mixed up with solid reality. I was heading for my own particular corner of the state, where I spent my boyhood, because I wanted to see what the years had done to it; and if in the end I learned more about what the years had done to me—well, that is what usually happens when you go on a pilgrimage.

My own land is mostly Benzie County, which has fewer inhabitants now than it had half a century ago but which has lost its old backwoods isolation and is a homey, friendly sort of country. There is a tiny town with the improbable name of Benzonia, which was founded by some eager folk from Oberlin College just before the Civil War when all of this land was new. The air was so clear and good that they wanted a name that would tell about it, so they dipped into their erudition and came up with a Latin-Greek hybrid which means, roughly, fragrant air. They built a little college, and for fifty years it struggled along, graduating eight or ten people a year; then it was turned into a preparatory school, and my father was principal of it when I was a boy, and just after World War I there was no longer any need for this school because the state's high schools had improved, and it quietly died. Nothing is left of it now except a brick building which has been turned into a village community house, but the little town drowses under the long sunlight, with a special flavor that other little towns don't have, touched by the memory of the old-timers who wanted to bring education to the lumber country.

Every man makes his own state—or maybe his state makes him; it is hard to be certain about such things. But you grow up with something on your mind, and it comes out of the place where you were born and reared, and you never can get away from it no matter where you go. And if you go back, long afterward, to the place you knew when you were young, you see it through eyes that were specially conditioned; you cannot be objective about it; you try to write about your background and find that you are really writing about yourself.

I remember, forty years ago, a January night when the thermometer registered five below and there was a brilliant full moon, and I went to the front door, late at night, to lock up. I stood in the doorway for a moment, looking out at the moonlit landscape, the little grove of trees across the street and the three feet of snow that covered everything. There is not in all America today anything quite as still and quiet as a Michigan small town could be, late on a moon-swept night, in January, in the days before World War I. Nobody in all the earth was making a sound, nothing was moving, there was only the white snow, the black trees, the blue shadows lying on the whiteness, and the big moon in a cloudless sky; and to stand there and look out at it was, inexplicably, to be in touch with the Infinite—and, somehow, the Infinite was good, it was lonely but friendly, it meant something you did not have to be afraid of if you understood it. So Michigan means that to me—along with

much else—and coldness and loneliness and shattering
loveliness go hand in hand, so that while you will always
be awed and abashed when you come up against the Infinite
you do not really need to be afraid. And maybe that is a
fairly good idea to get and take with you.

I can remember another night, in summertime, much
earlier, when as a rather small boy my family took me across
Lake Michigan on a steamboat from Milwaukee. It was dark
and cool and windy, and we came out of the river and out
past the breakwater, and the steamer began to rise and fall
on the waves of the big lake. For a small child it was quite
scary—nothing but water and the dark, with big waves
coming in from nowhere and making foaming noises under
the bow, and the Michigan shore seemed an unimaginable
distance away and the dark sea ahead was what all adventurers have always seen when they pitted themselves
against the great emptiness and its wonder and peril, and
life itself is an enormous gamble played by people who are
eager and frightened at the same time, with nothingness
before and above and the chance of a dawn-swept landfall
in the morning lying there, insubstantial and improbable
beyond the night, as the possible reward. That is really the
truth of it, and that too is good to know.

I am well aware, of course, that, as the world's seas go,
Lake Michigan is not really a very large body of water. To
cross it by steamer is to spend no more than half a dozen
hours afloat, and when the trip is over you have reached
only the state of Michigan, which actually is as prosaic a
bit of land as you can find. Yet the thoughts of a small boy
can be lonely, frightening and touched with unfathomable
wonder, and the borders of an unattainable land can glim-
mer, insubstantial but genuine, over the most matter-of-fact
horizon. What you owe the land where you were born and
reared is something you can never quite pin down; but if
that land can stir dreams and fears and the hints of a completely illogical but convincing promise, you are that much

ahead of the game. For what you think and feel when you are very small never quite leaves you, and if it always lures you on to something that the visible landscape does not quite make explicit you are immeasurably the gainer.

All of this means very little, probably, by any rational scheme of things. Yet somehow it is part of the color and the flavor which this strange, light-struck, improbable country gave to me when I was too young to know any better, and it has had its own queer effect on everything I have thought or done ever since. So I bring it in here, along with the pine trees and the cold winds and the everlasting golden sands, to try to explain why I like to go back to Michigan. I am probably trying to recapture something unattainable, but that does not matter; so long as the feel and the gleam of it still lie on the edge of my subconscious it is real, for me, and the only value in any dream consists in the fact that you have to keep pursuing it even though you know that you can never quite reach it. If the real Michigan keeps getting overlaid with the Michigan I thought I saw in the old days, I can only say that I am that much better off —for what I thought I saw then was worth a lifetime's quest.

There is plenty to see up here. Half a mile from this hilltop village is one of America's loveliest lakes—Crystal Lake, named with an utter literalness; it is so clear you can see the bottom where it is twenty feet deep—nine miles long by three miles wide, with wooded hills all around and a fringe of pleasant summer cottages along its sandy shores.

Crystal Lake itself will always be something special for me, because it symbolizes an emotion that goes beyond time and space. When I was very small the minister of the one church in my town of Benzonia took some months off, and—by dint of what patient frugality I do not know: the pastor of a country church at that time earned precious little money—made a trip to the Holy Land. When he returned he made his report, and of it I remember just one thing. The magical Sea of Galilee, he said, the sea where our Lord walked and taught and performed miracles, was just about the size and shape of our Crystal Lake. To be sure, the hills which bordered Galilee were dun-colored, barren of trees, a bleak and impoverished landscape; while our hills, green as the heart of a maple leaf, were ringed with clear water, set about with pleasant little towns, cool and pleasant, inviting people to linger on their long journey from one mystery to another. But the resemblance was there, and the lake in which I caught diminutive perch was very like the lake on which Peter tried to walk dry-shod; and for some reason my life is richer because a saintlike little pastor, half a century ago, saw Galilee through innocent eyes which could interpret any lake in terms of Michigan's pine trees and green open valleys. I have never been to Palestine, but somehow I have seen the Sea of Galilee, and the Word that was preached by that Near-Eastern sea has a special sound for me.

Over the range of hills at the western end of my Crystal Lake there is Lake Michigan itself, and where a little river cuts a channel through the high bluffs there is Frankfort, a summer-resort town and a busy little seaport as well. The Ann Arbor Railroad has its terminus here, with a fleet of car ferries that carry whole freight trains across Lake Michigan, and these big black steamers come and go at all hours of the day and night, 365 days a year. In the winter when the big lake is full of ice these boats often have quite a time of it, but they are sturdy icebreakers and they hack their way through regardless, although they sometimes make port with their upper works encased in ice.

From Frankfort you swing up toward Traverse City on route M 22, which cuts up across what is known as the Leelenau Peninsula. Once this was lumber country and now it is cherry country, but mostly it is a region for summer vacationers. Every little town has its lake (Glen Lake, which lies back of Sleeping Bear Point, is a show place) and there are other lakes with no towns at all, locked in by ice and snow for four or five months of the year.

Sleeping Bear Point is an enormous sand dune, five miles long by 500 feet high, jutting out into Lake Michigan. A road of sorts leads to the top, but your car would stall in the deep, fine sand, so you go to the town of Glen Haven and take passage in one of the special low-gear cars with over-sized, half-inflated tires, which waddle through the sand as if they were made for it. On the crest there is nothing at all to see but this golden empty ridge and the great blue plain of Lake Michigan far below, with white surf curling on the beach at the foot of the bluff, yet it is one of the finest sights in the Middle West. There is no noise except the lake wind ruffling the spare trees: there is just nothing except a feeling of infinite space and brightness, and utter freedom from the smoke and the rush and the racket of ordinary 20th Century life.

The country north of Traverse City is high and open, with Lake Michigan nearly always in view off to the left, and the little towns and villages along the way reflect the past in a curious manner. First there was the lumber era, in which today's sleepy hamlet was a rip-roaring little city with a solid mile of sawmills along the water front. Then, when the lumber was gone, there was the early summer-resort trade: passenger boats coming up from Chicago or around from Detroit; imposing but flimsy frame hotels, all veranda and white pillars, overlooking every beach; Pull-man cars unloading a new consignment of vacationers at the railroad depot every morning . . . and after a while the automobiles came and killed boat lines, passenger trains and most of the hotels, so that these towns which had made one readjustment had to make another. The result is odd. Every town contains echoes of those two vanished eras, and seems to be looking back regretfully to the past; and yet most of them are brighter and more hopeful than they ever were before, the old feeling of backwoods isolation is gone, the people who live here are having a better time of it than ever before and the general level of prosperity is higher and more stable. Yet the feeling of the past does linger, so that in this area which has hardly been settled more than a century there are haunting echoes of antiquity.

Your memory can play queer tricks on you. At Charlevoix I drove east, skirting the south shore of beautiful Lake Charlevoix to reach Boyne City. Boyne City was perhaps the last lumber boom town in the Lower Peninsula. We lived there, for a year or so, when I was about six years old, and it was a lively place then. There were four immense sawmills along the lake front, and a big "chemical plant" —I suppose it was a place where they extracted turpentine and other by-products from the pines—and there was even a blast furnace, although what it may have been doing there I have never been able to understand. Anyway, Boyne City was bustling and exciting, and our backyard ran down to the Boyne River, where the log drives came down in the spring. To my six-year-old eyes that river was immense; it was, I realized, probably smaller than the Mississippi, but it was fascinating, wide, turbulent, somehow menacing—a dangerous river which easily could (and, two or three times, very nearly did) drown a small boy who incautiously tried to play on its treacherous carpet of moving logs. So I returned to the old back yard and took another look at the river—and realized that either the river had shrunk or I had stretched considerably. The river is charming—gentle, crystal-clear, friendly, no more hostile than a brook. Along the lake front there is an uncommonly pleasant park, where the sawmills used to be. A rusted remnant of the old blast furnace still survives, but everything else seems to be gone; and this is not the exciting town where I used to live, it is just a bright, friendly little community where old memories are held in suspension in the sunlight.

Another of my favorite towns in this part of the state is Petoskey, where I was born. No man ever breaks completely away from his birthplace; you carry the mark of your home town with you. I remember it as a sleepy sort of place, built on a spectacular side hill that slants up steeply from the cold blue of Little Traverse Bay, with funny little tourist-bait shops at the bottom where Indian wares and other trinkets were offered for sale to the "summer people." These shops always smelled pleasantly of birch bark—there were baskets, and toy canoes, and other contrivances—and to this day the odor of birch bark takes me back to tiny stores which must have gone out of existence a whole generation ago.

Petoskey has grown up to date and prosperous. It is no longer a lumber center, and the great trains of flatcars piled high with pine logs no longer go rumbling past what used to be the Grand Rapids & Indiana depot, and the sprawling summer hotels I remember so well are not there any more; but because the hill is so high and because so much of the big lake lies open at the foot of the hill Petoskey gives you what so much of this part of Michigan always gives—the strange feeling that you are at an immense altitude, on some sort of ridge where you can look down on half of the Middle West and where the wind that never quite dies down has come to you without touching anything at all along the way from wherever it is that winds are born.

Even though it always speaks of the past, and seems to look back toward it in a dreamy sort of way, most of this part of Michigan has no particular history. But when you go north from Petoskey you step far back into legend and the distant past. Things were going on here when the eastern seaboard colonies were still young. La Salle, Jolliet and Marquette were here nearly three centuries ago. At Mackinaw City, at the very tip of Michigan's Lower Peninsula, and an hour's easy drive from Petoskey, there is a lake-front park with a rebuilt stockade which marks the site of one of early America's most significant strong points—Fort Michilimackinac. Here, around 1681, missionaries and fur traders and French soldiers and a scattering of just plain adventurers built an outpost of French civilization in a spot which was more remote and isolated than any spot on earth can be today.

After the French left Canada the British took over, and in 1763 Pontiac's painted warriors broke in, seized stockade and fort, and massacred the British garrison. Then the fort was abandoned, to be rebuilt on Mackinac Island, which lies in the center of the straits. The Americans took it over after the Revolution, and the British recaptured it in the War of 1812, and then it was returned to American possession again. Now it stands empty, a tourists' show place, looking out at the unending procession of freighters that cruise slowly past on their way to and from the lower lakes.

Mackinac Island is a delightful spot, and it is unusual in two ways. In the first place, although it is spelled Mackinac it is, for some incomprehensible reason, pronounced Mackinaw; and in the second place it is the one spot in the whole state of Michigan—one of the very few spots in all the United States—where you never see an automobile. Automobiles are not allowed on the island, and to come to this place, with its hotels and boardinghouses and curio shops lining the quiet streets, and the old-fashioned horse-drawn surreys leisurely wheeling their way in and out, is to step straight back into the Victorian era. To get about the island you walk, or ride behind a horse, or get on a bicycle. More so than any other place in the state, this is a refuge from the present.

Big changes are coming to Upper Michigan and the symbol of their approach is the stupendous five-mile-long bridge being built across the straits to connect the Lower and Upper Peninsula. The bridge will cost around $100,-000,000; it is expected to be completed this fall, and it will at last tie the two halves of the state firmly together. At present, you cross the straits by one of a fleet of state-owned ferry boats.

Michigan's Upper Peninsula is an immense finger of land running 300 miles from west to east, with cold, steely-blue Lake Superior, the largest lake in the world, lying all along its northern flank. Eighty-five per cent of this area is forested and lumbering is still going on, the Marquette iron range still turns out iron ore, and some copper is still being mined; but comparatively speaking the Upper Peninsula is almost empty, with fewer than 300,000 inhabitants. If the northern half of the Lower Peninsula is North Country the Upper Peninsula is the same thing at treble strength. It is traversed by excellent concrete roads, and you can drive for two hours without seeing a town, or anything that looks like permanent human habitation. For mile after mile there is nothing except clear blue lakes, vast areas of cut-over timber, forests which look as if nobody had ever taken an ax into them, and outcroppings of bleak rock. With Lake Superior so close this country has its own built-in air-conditioning; there is a sharp edge to the air, a feeling of unlimited space and quiet and peace, and that strange quality of half-ominous, half-friendly loneliness is with you all of the time. Once the bridge is finished, all of this will probably be watered down, but it can never be wholly destroyed. After all, up in this country there is nothing between you and the North Pole except a few thousand miles of totally empty land and water.

One of the interesting things to see up here is the canal at Sault Ste. Marie, whose big locks connect Lake Superior with the lower lakes. The Soo, as everybody calls it, is a lively little city during the eight months of the navigation season; it boasts that its canal handles more traffic than Panama and Suez combined. All day and all night the ships—enormous things, 500 and 600 feet in length—come majestically in from the upper lake, floating high above

your head, sinking slowly as the water burbles out of the
locks, and then gliding off for the great industrial region
hundreds of miles to the south. In an average day, eighty
or ninety of them will go through. Day and night, you are
forever hearing the deep, haunting bass of their whistles—
the inescapable, wholly characteristic and somehow deeply
romantic noise of the Soo region. (Progress is taking a
hand here, these immense boats are being equipped with
air horns, which emit a blatting which carries a great deal
farther than the traditional steam whistle but which is pure
discord and nothing more.)

Driving west from the Soo, on the broad highway that
leads to Marquette and the iron-range country, you pass
Seney, a drowsy little country town so unobtrusive that you
can go all the way through it before you realize you have
reached it. It's quiet and orderly today, but half a century
ago Seney was a hell-roaring lumber town, with a reputation for unrestrained misconduct that did not need to take
second place to any Western cattle town or mining camp.
There is a myth, formerly given wide circulation in the Sun-
day supplements, about a log stockade that once adorned
the town. In it, according to one version, dance-hall girls
were kept when not dancing; according to another, captive
lumberjacks were immured here between spells in the backwoods. There is one odd thing about these fancy yarns of
the high-wide-and-handsome days of the lumber towns;
the sins which were committed in these places were never
really attractive. It is very hard to glamorize a village
rowdy, and the lumberjack tough mugs were at bottom
village rowdies and nothing better. Seney's most notorious
character, for instance, was a loafer who used to win free
drinks in bars by biting the heads off frogs, mice and other
vermin. He finally came to a well-merited end, according to
the story, when he bit the head off a small owl which was
the particular pet of a burly lumberjack, who promptly
brought this unattractive character's career to a close by

smiting him vigorously over the head with the handle of a peavy.

Marquette is the metropolis of the Upper Peninsula. It is a solid industrial town, with red ore from the great ridges behind it coming down to the docks in red hopper cars, and if it is not the most lovely city in the United States it occupies one of the nation's most beautiful sites. The south shore of Lake Superior curves in and out, along here, with deep bays and jutting, pine-crowned headlands; the old primeval rock breaks through the crust of the land to remind you that this is the backbone of the continent, where rocks so ancient they even lack fossils lie bare under the long summer sunlight, grim and lonely and desolate. Just at sunset, from east of Marquette, you can see the city with the opaque blue panel of Lake Superior silent in front of it and a flaming red sky behind it, lying in the evening stillness like a dream of the city that never was; it is transfigured, a strange light lies on its towers and parapets, and this place that for so long was a Mecca for Cornish miners (the roadside stands still peddle Cornish pasties instead of hot dogs, and very good they are too) becomes an unattainable no-place out of fable, dropping long dark shadows on a silent cold sea.

If you are well-advised, you will head west from Marquette for the copper country. Do it, if possible, early in October when the lonely road will take you through forests aflame with scarlet and gold and bronze, and a wild, doomed beauty that belongs beyond the farthest edge of the world lies on all the landscape; the touch of everlasting winter is in the air and yet for an hour or so the sunlight is still warm, and nothing you will ever see will move you more or linger with you longer. You come out, at last, onto the long spine of the Keweenaw Peninsula—an outcrop of rock and wild trees, reaching far up into Lake Superior, perhaps the oldest land in the new world. The copper mines which caused men to come here in the first place go deep under the lake—some of the shafts go down for more than a mile. You get the feeling of a land that has been passed by, a hard, forbidding and strangely charming bit of country that had a short hectic history and does not especially want any more; and all about is the cold steely blue of the greatest of lakes, and the picturesque little settlements that manage to be both friendly and forsaken at the same moment.

It would be possible, of course, to drive on, noting the points of interest in the Upper Peninsula, mentioning the more unusual towns—like Eagle Harbor, one of the most completely beautiful villages I ever expect to see, with two long headlands enclosing a quiet strip of water and the great angry lake piling destructive surging waves against the rocks outside—but my state is half reality and half the dim, enchanted memories of a long-lost boyhood, and anyway I did not live in the entire state of Michigan. I knew only selected parts of it, and these parts stay in my memory and call back unforgettable things which were born of the cold emptiness and the inviting, menacing beauty of this North Country.

They are Upper Michigan, the part that lies north of the automobile belt, the doomed, bewitched country which presently will surrender to the Mackinac bridge and to the superhighway and which, ultimately, will undoubtedly become just another part of the sprawling, industrialized Middle West. But while today's light lasts it is still a land apart; there is a pleasantly melancholy flavor of a lost past to it, and although men murdered the forests with a passionate ferocity the forests somehow still live and put their strange touch on the countryside. There are cool shadows under the trees and a timeless peace lies on the cutover tracts and the fields where the young second growth is hiding the stumps.

It is a strange country: lonely enough, even in summer, and cold as the far side of the moon when winter comes, with the far-off hills rising pale blue from the frozen white landscape. It offers a chance to draw a deep breath, to turn around and look back at the traveled path, to stand on a high hill and be alone with the fresh air and the sunlight. It is wood and water, golden sand and blue lakes, emptiness and memories and the sort of isolation which it is hard for a city man to come by, these days. All in all, it is quite a state.